INNER WEALTH

FROM PAIN TO PURPOSE

HELEN HARRISON

Published in Australia by Helen Harrison

First published in Australia 2024
This edition published 2024
Copyright © Helen Harrison 2024
Typesetting: WorkingType (www.workingtype.com.au)
Cover Picture: Lauren Biggs Photography
Cover Design: Narelle Ellis NGirl Design

The right of Helen Harrison to be identified as the
Author of the Work has been asserted in accordance with the
Copyright, Designs and Patents Act 1988.

All rights reserved. No part of this publication may be reproduced, stored in a retrieval system, or transmitted, in any form or by any means without the prior written permission of the publisher, nor be otherwise circulated in any form of binding or cover other than that in which it is published and without a similar condition being imposed on the subsequent purchaser.

 A catalogue record for this book is available from the National Library of Australia

ISBN Paperback 978-0-6486224-1-3
ISBN Ebook 978-0-6486224-3-7

Disclaimer: The intent of the author is to offer information of a general nature to help you in your quest for emotional, spiritual, physical and mental well-being. In the event you use the information in this book for yourself, which is your constitutional right, the author and publisher

*For the courageous hearts who understand that
finding yourself is the greatest journey,
and healing is the greatest gift.*

Contents

Foreword		1
Chapter 1	Family	5
Chapter 2	Owen	15
Chapter 3	Lily	29
Chapter 4	Growing Up	44
Chapter 5	Leaving Home	66
Chapter 6	Losing Owen	78
Chapter 7	Security before Self	88
Chapter 8	A Family of My Own	98
Chapter 9	Shifting Sands	109
Chapter 10	Meeting Myself	128
Chapter 11	Giving Out Instead of Giving In	142
Chapter 12	Mother and Marriage	153
Chapter 13	A Milestone	168
Chapter 14	Spending Addiction	180
Chapter 15	Sexual Awakening	195
Chapter 16	Losing Lily	211
Chapter 17	Soul Awakening	224
Chapter 18	Inner Wealth	234
Author Bio		245

Foreword

Belonging is a primal yearning that's resonated within me since the dawn of my consciousness. It whispers quietly in the back of my mind, echoing throughout my life with a persistent question: "Where do I belong?" In the pages ahead, I share the reality of my story, driven by the constant search for belonging, haunted by the fear of abandonment, and brightened by breaking free of stereotypes.

I write with raw honesty and open vulnerability. I share the times of longing and searching, the silent cries of a soul trying to find its place in the world. Deep down in my heart, I wrestled with a constant feeling of not being good enough and a relentless chorus of self-doubt that threatened to swallow me whole.

As a kid, I felt the sting of not fitting in, the awkwardness of being different. I was that quiet one, always on the sidelines, watching and wondering where I belonged. The spectre of abandonment wasn't just a fear; it was a lived reality, shaping my every interaction and perception.

During my teenage years, things didn't get any easier. The search for identity and belonging became more desperate, more consuming. I faced the turbulence of peer pressure, the chaos of self-discovery, and the constant struggle to carve out a space where I felt seen and understood. It was a time of silent battles and loud defeats, where every rejection echoed louder and every acceptance felt like a fleeting dream.

But in these struggles, I found strength. Each setback taught me resilience, each moment of doubt pushed me to dig deeper. The need to belong became not just about finding my place in the world, but about creating it for myself. I learned to overthrow the stereotypes that sought to define me, to rise above the labels that tried to confine me and to follow my heart towards a life of inner peace and happiness.

As humans, we are wired for connection. All we want is to belong, to be seen and to be heard. Yet, for those of us who have felt the sting of rejection and the ache of loneliness, the pathway towards belonging can feel like an uphill battle. We internalise the messages of our perceived inadequacy and the belief that we are unworthy of love and acceptance.

For me, writing this book and launching it was confronting and emotional. Every rejection and negative feedback felt like a confirmation of my worst fears, reinforcing the idea that I was somehow less than others. I had to confront the shadows of my past, to face the pain I had buried so deeply. It was a painful process, unearthing wounds that had long festered, but it was also liberating. I know my worth isn't determined by others' acceptance but by my own self-acceptance.

This book allowed me to continue to cultivate self-compassion, to forgive myself for my perceived flaws and to embrace my true self, warts and all. This shift in perspective was transformative. In my life and in my book, I stopped seeking validation from others and started to find it within myself. The shame that had once weighed me down began to lift, replaced by a sense of self-worth and belonging. I know that the path to healing begins with self-compassion, with extending to ourselves the same kindness and understanding that we so readily offer to others. It is a path of acceptance, of awakening, of authenticity that promises not only to illuminate the path to self-discovery but also to lead us home, to the place where we truly belong within ourselves.

It is my own story from my own perspective and a testament to the resilience of the human spirit and its capacity for transformation. It is a path of awareness, acceptance and authentic action that promises not only to illuminate the way to self-discovery but also to lead us home, to the place where we truly belong and value our own self-worth. Through the challenge of adversity, I emerged with an unyielding resolve to challenge the rigid confines of societal norms and reclaim the fractured pieces of my identity.

I didn't want to get to the end of my life and realise I never did what I truly wanted. I wanted to write my life's story. I couldn't let fear hold me back. If this book saves even one life, I've done my job. Lily's spirit is within me, helping me face my fears and get this story out there. Lily has given me courage.

"Inner Wealth" isn't just my story; it's a testament to the power of vulnerability, the courage to face our deepest fears, and the relentless pursuit of authenticity. It's about finding light in the darkest corners of our experiences and using that light to guide us toward a richer, more meaningful existence. I wrote it from a soulful place, driven by a calling to explore how the push of pain and the pull of purpose have shaped my life. We've all got our traumas. Mine include experiences of adoption, sibling suicides, and the breakdown of my marriage. These events led me to transform inner turmoil into fulfilment. This book is my way of helping others navigate their trauma.

By sharing my story, I aim to inspire you to use your pain as a catalyst for growth and to find purpose and authenticity amidst life's challenges. Fear of rejection is something we all grapple with. Overcoming this fear can pave the way for purposeful living and reveal your true calling. "Inner Wealth" is about cultivating Awareness, Acceptance, and Authentic Action. I hope this book reaches the people who need it the most.

— **Helen Harrison**

Chapter 1

Family

As I look back on my childhood, the first thing I am struck by is the paradox of motherhood. Conditional love and deep-seated wounds shaped the landscape of my family life. From the very outset, my entry into this world was marked by struggle and uncertainty. The labour was fraught with difficulties. I was diagnosed with cerebral palsy. A mild form, the doctors assured my adopted parents, but one that would shape the trajectory of my life in ways I could not yet comprehend. Living with cerebral palsy was like navigating a labyrinth. It has been a maze of physical limitations and societal expectations that threatened to consume me.

My adopted mother, a teacher by profession, was committed to helping me live a normal life. I vividly recall the countless hours she spent with me, patiently coaxing me to read, even when every fibre of my being rebelled against the effort. It was a Herculean task. Perhaps she helped me tap into a determination that stayed with me for the rest of my life. Despite her best efforts, there were moments when the weight of my condition threatened to overwhelm us both. The simple act of pronouncing words and walking became a huge task. Each day felt like a daily struggle against the confines of my own body. My mother turned to the medical professionals for guidance, seeking support in the hope of a cure. But the advice they offered was not what she had expected. Instead of offering a glimmer of hope, they urged caution, warning against the perils of rushing into adoption and suggesting she give me back!!

As a toddler, I was described as a lovely baby. I would like to think I was a source of joy and delight for my parents amidst the chaos of our bustling household. However, despite my sunny disposition, it quickly became apparent as my development lagged that of my peers, was I a burden on my parents? While other children my age were taking their first tentative steps and babbling excitedly, I struggled to reach simple milestones. Walking, talking, and all the typical markers of childhood development were delayed. Yet, despite having these challenges, I remained a contented little soul, blissfully unaware of the hurdles that lay ahead.

It's important to note the context of my upbringing. My parents already had three biological children of their own, each with their own unique needs and personalities. In addition, they had previously adopted a child who also faced significant challenges. She was a child who was not only profoundly deaf, but also battled heart problems, developmentally delayed and required a feeding tube for the first 18 months of her life. Amid caring for a child with such complex needs, my own delays may have seemed like just another drop in the ocean of parental responsibilities.

Perhaps the most painful aspect of my early years was the taunts and jeers that echoed through the halls of my childhood. "Watermelon," they called me, mocking my perceived disproportionality. I had a big head atop a small body, a visual reminder of my perceived otherness. In those moments, I felt the sting of rejection like a dagger to the heart. It was a wound that cut deep into the very core of my being. I longed to belong, to be accepted for who I was, but instead, I found myself cast adrift in a sea of indifference, struggling to find my place in a world that seemed determined to push me aside.

Growing up, I felt a constant, unbridgeable distance between Mum and me. Her love, while fierce and protective, was often overshadowed by her own unresolved trauma. There were moments when her pain would surface, casting a long, dark shadow over our home. Her inability to connect with me on a deeper level left me feeling isolated and yearning for a bond that never fully materialised.

My adopted mother, a woman of sacrifice and resilience, bore the scars of her own upbringing like badges of honour, each one a testament to the trials she had endured. She was raised as an only child in the tumultuous aftermath of World War II. Her childhood was marked by hardship and adversity, growing up in the shadow of conflict, her world shaped by the echoes of bombings and air raid sirens. Trauma deeply affects the central nervous system, causing chronic stress responses, heightened sensitivity, and ongoing triggers throughout one's life. Yet, amidst the chaos and uncertainty, she found little relief in the embrace of her own mother, who was the matron at her boarding school. She wasn't allowed to call her mum; instead, she had to refer to her as "Mrs." and treat her like any other teacher.

It was a legacy of pain passed down through generations like a silent inheritance. She spoke of her childhood with a mixture of longing and resentment, recounting tales of dormitories and strict matrons, of loneliness and isolation. Her relationship with her own mother was fraught with tension, a delicate dance of love and resentment that left its mark on her soul. When it came time for her to become a mother, she carried with her the weight of her own wounds; the scars of a childhood marked by abandonment and longing.

I can only imagine the confusion and isolation she must have felt, unable to receive the maternal affection she so desperately needed. How could she have showed me the love and nurturing I yearned for if she had never received it herself? I searched for validation in her eyes, yearning for acceptance, yet always feeling like I fell short. Mum's resilience was both a blessing and a curse. Her strength, while admirable, became a barrier to our connection. She was tough, no doubt about it. She had a way of pushing through adversity that was both awe-inspiring and, at times, intimidating. Our interactions were often strained, filled with unspoken words and unmet needs. The more I tried to bridge the gap between us, the more I felt her pulling away, unable to give what she had never received.

With three biological children of her own and seven more mixed culture adoptions into the fold, our family was a testament to my mother's boundless capacity for sacrifice rather than love. As we grew older, the challenges of motherhood became increasingly apparent. Babies, she would often say, give you unconditional love. They are pure, innocent and untouched by the weariness of the world. But as they grow, they begin to test the limits of that love, pushing back against the boundaries set by their parents. Eventually peeling away from that absolute adoration, individuality begins and independence follows, leaving a gaping void. She struggled to find her footing as we got older, grappling with the complexities of raising children in a world that seemed determined to challenge everything she was bought up to believe.

My earliest memories are like fragmented pieces of a patchwork quilt, each one woven with threads of lack and longing. One such memory takes me back to Sundays, when the scent of freshly ironed fabric hung in the air like a comforting embrace. It was a ritual in our household, my mother diligently smoothing out every crease with precision. As she worked, her hands moving rhythmically across the fabric, she would often pause to talk to me. It was one of the times I can remember the warmth in my mother's words.

We moved many times, but the Sunday ritual stayed the same and provided a sense of security amidst uncertainty. One of the houses we lived in was at Pakowhai Road in Hastings, Hawke's Bay, New Zealand. Within the confines of our garden, I found a sanctuary. For me, it was my first haven of greenery and solitude. There, beneath the shade of a towering tree, I would lose myself in a world of wonder and imagination. The earth beneath my feet was soft and yielding, a testament to the nurturing embrace of Mother Nature herself. In those moments, I felt a connection to the natural world, as if the very soil whispered secrets of belonging and acceptance. Nature was my mother.

I learned to find calm in her embrace and to seek refuge amidst the branches that danced in the gentle breeze. It was a place where I felt safe, where the worries of the world seemed to fade into insignificance. In the quiet rustle of leaves and the symphony of bird songs, I discovered a sense of belonging that transcended the confines of human interaction. Many times, this connection to the earth was what saved me.

Beyond the haven of our garden lay a world fraught with challenges and uncertainties. We moved frequently, our family expanding with each new adopted child. Yet, with each change of address came a sense of displacement. I had a constant feeling of being uprooted from the familiar and thrust into the unknown. My need for structure and certainty was never acknowledged or met in the way I needed it to be in order to feel safe.

I often think back to the different places we lived, each one leaving an indelible mark on my memories. One particular home stands out, where a majestic walnut tree stood sentinel in the back yard, its branches reaching skyward like outstretched arms. It was a sanctuary of sorts, a refuge from the chaos of the world outside. Outside the house, in the embrace of nature, was the only place where I felt safe and loved. I spent countless hours beneath the shade of that tree, my hands stained with the earthy scent of crushed walnuts. In those moments, I was not just a child; I was a part of something greater. I was a part of the intricate web of life that bound us all together.

My love for spending time outdoors wasn't just a preference; it was a necessity born out of our circumstances. Growing up in a house full of energetic kids, the walls often felt like they were closing in on us, stifling and suffocating. But outside, under the vast New Zealand sky, we were free. Free to roam and explore, to let our imaginations run wild. Out there, we felt like we belonged, even if just for a moment and only in our minds. It was enough for me, but not for everyone.

The backyard became our playground, and the garden our kingdom. We'd climb ancient pōhutukawa trees, chase each other around bushes dotted throughout the lawn, and invent games that could last for hours. The outdoors offered a sense of freedom we couldn't find inside. The feeling of the sun on our skin, the crisp scent of the freshly mowed grass mixed with the earthy aroma of native ferns, and the sound of tūī birds calling from the treetops. It was all a kind of magic.

On family outings we'd pile out of the car, eager to explore. The gardens we visited for family picnics were the playground perfect for games of hide and seek. Among the twists and turns of the pathways, we'd hide behind tall hedges, under ancient trees, and in secret corners, giggling with excitement as we evaded our seekers. The rush of adrenaline as I sprinted through the gardens, the thrill of finding the perfect hiding spot, and the sheer joy of being outdoors, feeling the sun on my face and the wind in my hair was pure joy.

Between games, we'd spread out on a blanket Dad laid out, nestled under the shade of a grand old tree. The sandwiches tasted even better outdoors, surrounded by the beauty of nature and the laughter of family. Those picnics were more than just meals in the park. They were moments of connection and joy. They taught us the simple pleasure of being together, of exploring the natural world, and of cherishing each other's company. Even now, the smell of freshly cut grass or the taste of a homemade sandwich brings back those cherished memories of carefree days in Napier Botanical Gardens.

For me, those moments were a lifeline. They gave me space to breathe, to dream and to just be. But not everyone in our household felt the same way. Some of my siblings struggled to find the same sense of belonging outside. For them, the open sky didn't provide the same escape; their struggles followed them wherever they went. The outdoors couldn't erase the challenges we faced at home, but it offered a temporary refuge, a place where at least some of us could find a bit of peace.

Looking back, I realise how much time spent in nature shaped me. It taught me resilience, sparked my creativity, and gave me a deep appreciation for the natural world.

Even now, when life feels overwhelming, I find peace and purpose in nature. It's where I feel most at home, most myself. The landscapes of New Zealand, with their raw beauty and endless horizons, continue to be my refuge, a reminder of the boundless freedom I found in those childhood days, even if it was only in my mind.

Healing in Practice

Grounding, also known as earthing, is a therapeutic technique that involves activities designed to "ground" or electrically reconnect you to the earth. This practice is rooted in earthing science and grounding physics, which explain how electrical charges from the earth can positively affect your body. The idea behind grounding is simple: by making direct physical contact with the earth—whether through walking barefoot on grass, soil, or sand, or immersing yourself in water—you allow your body to absorb the earth's natural electrons. These electrons are thought to act as antioxidants, helping to neutralize free radicals and reduce inflammation in the body.

Grounding can be done in various ways:
- Walking Barefoot: One of the most common and simplest methods, walking barefoot on natural surfaces like grass, sand, or soil can immediately reconnect you with the earth.
- Grounding Mats and Sheets: These specially designed products can be used indoors to simulate the effects of direct contact with the earth.

- Water Immersion: Submerging yourself in natural bodies of water, such as lakes, rivers, or the sea, can also provide grounding benefits.

Research suggests that grounding may help improve sleep, reduce pain and inflammation, enhance mood, and promote overall well-being. The theory is that by aligning our body's electrical potential with that of the earth, we can restore balance to our body's bioelectrical systems.

Grounding taps into a fundamental aspect of our relationship with the natural world. In our modern, technology-driven lives, we often become disconnected from the earth's energy. Grounding offers a simple, yet powerful way to restore that connection, promoting physical and emotional health. By incorporating grounding into your daily routine, you can experience the benefits of this natural practice, enhancing your overall sense of well-being and reinforcing your connection to the earth.

Self-Assessment Questions

How do you think your parent's own upbringing and childhood experiences impacted their approach to parenting and their relationship with you?

What role do you believe nature and outdoor spaces play in providing peace and a sense of belonging for you?

What shared family rituals and routines did you do as a child that contributed to your sense of security and connection and what do you do now?

Chapter 2

Owen

When I was two years old, our family welcomed a new little boy. Owen, a Tongan boy, would irrevocably alter the dynamics of our household. As he came quietly into our lives, he brought with him a significant cultural heritage and a unique set of experiences that set him apart from the rest of us.

Owen was unlike anyone I had ever known. From a very young age, he was reserved and introspective, with a quiet demeanour that seemed to conceal what was going on behind his sad eyes. From the moment he arrived, it was clear that he was different, not just in appearance, but in temperament and disposition as well.

I remember watching him with curiosity, trying to understand this new brother who was so unlike the rest of us. We were a boisterous, lively bunch, always up for a bit of rough-and-tumble, but Owen was different. He preferred to sit quietly, observing rather than participating in our chaotic games. His presence brought a calmness to the house that was both intriguing and unsettling. As a young child, I struggled to understand Owen's introverted nature. It was as if he inhabited a separate world that existed parallel to our own, yet remained elusive and inaccessible to me. I played beside him, but not with him. He didn't connect with things like I did. He stayed apart. Other.

In the eyes of my parents, Owen's introversion was a source of concern. Any deviation from the norm that threatened to disrupt the delicate balance of our family dynamics was in their eyes cause for disdain and distrust. While they had initially welcomed him into our home with open arms, there was an undercurrent of unease that lingered beneath the surface as he grew older. They subconsciously or otherwise perpetrated a subtle tension that coloured all our interactions with him.

Looking back, I can't help but wonder why Owen was treated differently from the rest of us. Was it simply a matter of personality clashes, unconscious parenting deficiencies or were there deeper underlying issues at play? Perhaps it was his Tongan heritage that clashed with the predominantly Pākehā (white New Zealander) environment in which we were raised. Or maybe it was his introverted nature which was a trait that my parents struggled to understand and accept. Whatever the reason, the treatment Owen received at the hands of my parents was nothing short of heartbreaking and confusing. He was often overlooked and marginalized, relegated to the fringes of our family dynamic. It was a subtle form of discrimination and one that was perhaps not overtly malicious, but damaging nonetheless. I am filled with a sense of sadness and regret. He deserved so much more than what he received.

To me, he was just another member of our family. My little brother to be loved and accepted unconditionally. Without meaning to, he shone a light on the subtle biases and prejudices by just being himself. He never had a chance to be embraced for who he was. As I grew older, I began to see the cracks in our family façade.

As a child with nine siblings, hunger was our constant companion. We had a gnawing physical and emotional emptiness that plagued us day and night. "Why am I always hungry?" I would ask myself. The truth was simple: there was not enough food to go around. This caused me so much shame. No one at school knew we were hungry. So, help never came.

In our household, food became a weapon. It became a tool used by my parents to exert control and discipline. If I had misbehaved, I would be sent to bed with no dinner. Sleeping on an empty stomach was difficult. The weekly menu was a rigid schedule of meagre offerings, each day's fare carefully rationed to eke out what little sustenance we had. I remember Monday was porridge, Tuesday was two slices of toast and Wednesday was a small bowl of cereal. The monotony of the menu was suffocating and a stark reminder of our precarious existence.

The lack of food in our house wasn't just about being short on cash. It went deeper than that. My parents, both raised in the post-war era, had grown used to a life of scarcity and deprivation. They knew hunger all too well, having lived through times when food was a luxury, not a given. For Mum, food wasn't just about keeping us fed. It was something precious, to be hoarded and rationed. It was a throwback to those hard days of her childhood, shaped by the trauma of war and the constant fear of not having enough to eat. This fear left a mark on her, and she passed it down to us through her tight control over our limited food supply.

Every meal was an exercise in stretching things as far as they could go. Leftovers were never wasted, and every crumb was counted. Mum's stories of ration books and the struggle to put food on the table made it clear why she was so strict. She'd tell us about queuing for bread and how a decent meal was a rare treat. These tales, filled with echoes of hardship, painted a picture of a time when just getting by was a victory.

I remember the pantry shelves lined with tins of baked beans and spaghetti, each can a small victory against the fear of going without. Fresh piece of lamb roast was a rarity, saved for special occasions. Our garden became a little oasis of self-sufficiency, with Dad teaching us to grow veggies to supplement our diet. It was here I first learned the value of food and the hard work that went into producing it.

Dad was the same as Mum. His stories of growing up with hand-me-downs and making do with what little they had stuck with us. He'd laugh about the ingenuity needed to stretch a meal for a family of seven, but there was always an undertone of seriousness, a reminder of ever-present scarcity. Even though times had changed, and we weren't as poor as their

Chapter 2 Owen

parents had been, the mindset lingered. It was a way of life, a lens through which they viewed the world. And in a way, it grounded us. It taught us resilience and the importance of being resourceful. But it also meant that I was always hungry.

In the absence of enough food to satisfy my hunger, I turned to desperate measures to squash the gnawing emptiness inside me. Stealing became a means of survival and a way to supplement our rations with whatever scraps I could find. In the dead of night, I would often find myself creeping out of bed and tiptoeing into the kitchen, on a mission to satisfy the gnawing pain in my belly that kept me awake. The darkness shrouded my movements as I navigated the familiar terrain of our home, and my footsteps were muffled by the carpet beneath my feet. I would make my way, quietly and carefully, past the Welsh dresser. It was an imposing piece of furniture that loomed large near my bedroom, on the way to the kitchen and the biscuit tin.

With trembling hands, I'd carefully select a biscuit, just one, to avoid detection. Each crumbly piece promised a momentary reprieve from the hunger that tore at my insides and a fleeting taste of sweetness in a world that held little comfort. But even as I ate, a nagging sense of guilt gnawed at the edges of my conscience. I knew that what I was doing was wrong. I was betraying the trust of my parents and flouting the rules that governed our household. Yet, in that moment, the allure of the forbidden proved too powerful to resist.

I'd savour each bite, letting the sweet crumbs dissolve

slowly on my tongue, trying to stretch out the pleasure as long as possible. It was a small rebellion, a quiet act of defiance in a world where food was rationed, and every mouthful was accounted for. The thrill of sneaking that biscuit was almost as satisfying as the taste itself, a secret indulgence that was mine alone. But the guilt was always there, lurking in the background. I'd hear Mum's voice in my head, warning us about the importance of saving every scrap, of never wasting a single bite. Mother Teresa's picture in the dining room looming over us. The fear of being caught, of seeing the disappointment in her eyes, was a constant companion. Yet, despite the fear and guilt, I couldn't stop myself. Those stolen moments of sweetness were a rare escape from the strict controlled confines of our daily life.

Afterwards, I'd carefully wipe away any crumbs, making sure there was no evidence of my little crime, my heart pounding as I listened for any signs that I'd been discovered. The rush of adrenaline, the mix of satisfaction and shame. It was a familiar cycle, one that I couldn't seem to break.

Even now, thinking back to those days, I can still taste the sweetness of those biscuits and feel the weight of the guilt that came with them. They were a small comfort in a tough world, a stolen pleasure that carried the burden of secrecy. But they also taught me about the complexities of hunger and desire, about the lengths we'll go to for a taste of something more.

One morning, my deceit was discovered. Dad burst into the room, a mixture of anger and disappointment on his face as he confronted us all about the pilfered biscuits. In his eyes,

Chapter 2 Owen

our transgression was a personal betrayal. It was a breach of trust that demanded swift retribution. With a sinking heart, I watched as he meticulously inspected each bed, searching for evidence of the night's forbidden activities. Owen, unbeknownst to me, had fallen victim to the same temptation and his bed betrayed the telltale crumbs. I couldn't help but feel a pang of guilt at Owen's predicament. Though I had been spared the brunt of Dad's anger, I knew that my silence played a role in Owen's punishment which consisted of having to go to bed early, missing a meal and the withdrawal of communication which I called the silent treatment. Yet, in that moment, self-preservation outweighed any sense of loyalty or justice.

Looking back on those early years, I can't help but feel a wave of unease. The memory of constant hunger is like a ghost that still haunts me. Going to bed with an empty stomach night after night is a cruel fate, one that left a permanent mark on me. It was a scar that never really faded. It wasn't just the physical sensation of hunger that marked me; it was the feeling of helplessness, the anxiety that came with not knowing when my most basic needs would be met, and it shaped me in ways I didn't fully understand until I was older. For a long time, I found myself overbuying groceries, always carrying snacks with me, panicking if I felt hungry or feeling uneasy if the pantry wasn't well-stocked. It was a habit that was hard to break.

Owen and I would head out on our daily walk to primary school, our footsteps the only sound in the quiet morning air. We didn't talk much. Along the way, we'd pass rows of rubbish bins, their contents like an irresistible source of discarded scraps and leftovers. It was here, among other people's rubbish, that we'd scavenge for something to eat. We'd quickly grab what we could, hoping to find something half-decent before anyone noticed. It was purely a matter of survival, and in those moments, we were just two kids trying to make it through the day.

As I reflect on those long walks to school, a sense of sadness washes over me. To hunger is to suffer. Together, my brother and I forged a bond forged in hardship. It was a silent understanding that transcended words. We found comfort in each other's company. Our strange special sort of togetherness became a beacon of hope amidst the darkness that threatened to consume me. But as the years wore on, the desperation only grew. It felt as though the relentless hunger picked away at the edges of our sanity.

At school, I would make excuses to retreat to the solitude of the bathroom so I could get out of class, my hands trembling as I rifled through the lunchboxes of my classmates. There always remained a veil of secrecy and a silent pact of shame that bound me to my suffering. No one knew of the hunger or the desperation that drove me to such desperate measures. It was a burden Owen and I bore together, but alone. To this day, I don't think anyone knew. If they did, they never knew the extent to which we were neglected.

There was a box tucked away in a forgotten corner of the primary school which was a keeper of lost treasures. Yellow envelopes contained a coin or two, when in a moment of fleeting honesty, someone had turned it in. I remember the day I discovered those envelopes, located near the sick bay. I stole them. My hands trembling with guilt, I stuffed them into my pockets. Once emptied of the coins and notes, I hid most of the envelopes away in a makeshift grave at the end of a friend's driveway in a futile attempt to hide what I had done. I went to the shop and bought food for me and Owen. Guilt lingered, a heavy weight upon my soul, as I struggled to reconcile my actions with the person I wanted to be.

Because I was late home from school, my mum checked my school bag and found the rest of the yellow envelopes. That afternoon, I found myself sitting in the principal's office, my father by my side. Mr. Hill, with his gentle voice and kind eyes, asked, "Why did you do it?" And though I longed to confess and to lay bare the truth of my suffering, I remained silent, my shame a barrier that I could not overcome. I had the opportunity to speak my truth, to share the burden of my hunger, but I let it slip away, under a cloud of self-doubt and self-recrimination. I couldn't condemn my father. It was my shame to bear.

And it wasn't just hunger. I vividly recall the bitter chill of New Zealand winters, the biting wind that seeped through the cracks in our uninsulated home. My nights were spent shivering under threadbare blankets, leaving me yearning for warmth and security. There were early mornings when the cold seemed to seep into my bones, leaving me trembling and desperate for reprieve. In those moments, all I longed for was the simple comfort of a warm jacket to wear to school, a barrier against the biting cold that threatened to consume me.

But even as I grappled with these physical hardships, there were subtler forms of deprivation that weighed heavily on my young shoulders. The absence of clean sheets, the lack of basic hygiene and other indignities that marked my daily existence. In a household plagued by scarcity, even the most basic of comforts were often out of reach. My parents, burdened by their own struggles, were unable to provide for our most fundamental needs. Their obsession with scarcity and sacrifice scarred my life, leaving me to fend for myself in a world that seemed determined to break me. I still sometimes ask myself where that determination came from and why I am the one still here.

Maslow's Hierarchy of Needs is a psychological theory that outlines the five basic levels of human needs, arranged in a pyramid. At the base of this pyramid lie the fundamental requirements for survival such as food, water, and shelter. As I reflect on my childhood, I realize how deeply linked my formative years were intertwined with the ingrained trauma I have spent years trying to heal. I grew up with my basic needs not being met. I wasn't the only one.

Healing in Practice
Building trust after a childhood where love was limited is like tending a delicate garden. It starts with small interactions, like sharing a bit about your weekend with new friends or colleagues, and seeing if they respond with genuine interest.

Slowly, these small exchanges grow into reliable support systems.

You look for relationships where there's open communication and mutual respect, finding comfort in conversations where you're truly understood. For instance, having a mate who listens without judgment when you talk about your bad day, or a colleague who respects your opinion in meetings.

Therapy can be a game-changer, providing a safe space to explore your fears and anxieties. It's like having a skilled gardener to help you understand why certain plants (or feelings) need more care. Self-compassion is crucial too, reminding you to be patient with your progress, like giving yourself time to grow.

Gradually, you learn to set and enforce boundaries, which creates a sense of safety. For example, saying no to social plans when you need some downtime, or speaking up when someone crosses a line. Over time, you start to understand your triggers and communicate your needs more effectively. Maybe you realise that certain situations make you anxious, and you learn to avoid or prepare for them.

Each small step forward is a victory, building a foundation of trust with yourself and others. Eventually, trust blossoms, allowing you to form deeper, more meaningful connections. It's a slow process, but like a well-tended garden, the effort pays off, creating your own inner wealth and a network of strong, supportive relationships.

Examples of building trust with yourself and others:

Small Interactions

- Sharing Minor Details: Start by telling a new friend about your favourite hobby or weekend plans and see if they show genuine interest.
- Listening and Responding: If someone shares something with you, listen actively and respond thoughtfully. This builds a reciprocal trust.

Reliable Support

- Consistent Actions: Notice if a friend consistently shows up when they say they will, like meeting you for a weekly coffee catch-up.
- Acts of Kindness: Small gestures like a friend offering to help you move house or bring you soup when you're sick.

Open Communication

- Honest Conversations: Have a heart-to-heart with a friend about something that's been bothering you and see if they listen and offer support.
- Mutual Respect: If a friend respects your boundaries, such as understanding when you need alone time.

Self-Compassion

- Being Patient: Remind yourself that building trust takes time, just like learning a new skill.

- Celebrating Progress: Acknowledge small victories, like feeling comfortable enough to share a personal story with someone.

Setting Boundaries
- Saying No: Politely decline social invitations when you need to recharge.
- Expressing Needs: Letting a friend know if their teasing crosses a line and makes you uncomfortable.

Understanding Triggers
- Identifying Anxiety: Recognising that large crowds make you anxious and planning accordingly by choosing quieter hangout spots.
- Communicating Needs: Telling a partner that you need reassurance after an argument because of past experiences.

Deeper Connections
- Shared Experiences: Planning a trip with friends and trusting them to handle parts of the journey.
- Emotional Support: Feeling comfortable enough to cry in front of a close friend or family member and receiving comfort without feeling judged.

Self-Assessment Questions

Have you ever felt compelled to keep a secret because of shame or fear of judgment? How did carrying that secret affect you emotionally and mentally?

Think about how not having enough of something essential influenced your feelings of self-worth and how you interacted with others.

Have you ever had to overcome significant challenges due to a lack of support from those around you? What do you think fuelled your determination to persevere, and how has this resilience impacted your life?

Chapter 3

Lily

It must have been around the age of seven or eight when affection had seemed to vanish from our household. There were so many children needing love yet it wasn't just scarce, it was non-existent. In a home with parents who were the epitome of emotional detachment, I often felt like I was not only starving for food, but for love. When I was ten, my life took a dramatic turn with the arrival of baby Erolini, or Lily as we fondly called her. I vividly remember the anticipation that buzzed through our home as we eagerly awaited her arrival. It was a breath of fresh air amid the rigours of our everyday routine. Then, one day, she arrived. She was a tiny bundle of joy, swaddled in blankets, her almond-shaped eyes gleaming with innocence and wonder.

I still remember the first moment I saw her. I walked into the lounge room after a long day at school, and there she was, nestled in the crook of Mum's arms. Her black curly hair framed her cherubic face perfectly. In that instant, something inside me shifted. A sense of love and protectiveness washed over me like a tidal wave. From that day on, Lily became my constant companion, my little mate, and my source of joy and comfort in a world full of uncertainties.

I'll never forget the day of Lily's baptism. There I was, standing in the church, clutching her chubby little body in my arms. I was only ten years old at the time, a skinny, awkward kid with a head that still felt too big for my body. Tasked with holding this big Samoan baby in front of the entire congregation, I felt both pride and anxiety. I'd only been allowed a single piece of toast and one egg for breakfast. But despite my hunger, I had a more pressing concern.

She was a hefty little thing, her chubby cheeks and plump limbs making her seem even larger than she was. As I stood there in my handmade dress by Mum, struggling to support her weight, I felt overwhelmed by the task at hand. My arms ached from the strain, and I longed to be free of the burden. But I couldn't show weakness, not in front of the congregation and not in front of my family. I gritted my teeth and bore the discomfort silently, my eyes darting nervously around the church. Just when I thought I couldn't bear it any longer, my father shot me a pointed look. It was a silent rebuke to toughen up and fulfil my duty as Lily's godmother. I swallowed back my tears and straightened my shoulders, determined to endure whatever hardships lay ahead. Despite my resolve, I couldn't shake the feeling of inadequacy. Here I was, a mere child, burdened with responsibilities far beyond my years, and I couldn't help but wonder if I was up to the task.

Yet, as I stood there, my arms aching and my stomach

Chapter 3 Lily

growling, for the first time I felt like I was not alone. As her godmother, I felt a deep sense of responsibility towards her and a commitment to nurture and protect her with all my heart. It wasn't just the title of godmother that bound us together. It was something deeper and more profound. It was a soul connection that transcended words or labels and a bond forged in the crucible of love and shared experience. In that sacred moment, I realised that my love and dedication would see me through any challenge. I held her close, feeling her steady breathing and the warmth of her body against mine. It was then that I knew, despite my fears and doubts, that I was ready to embrace the role of godmother with all the strength and love I had to offer.

When we grew older, Lily became more than just a baby sister. She became my confidante, my cuddle buddy and my closest ally in the battle against adversity. Together, we navigated the trials and tribulations of childhood, sharing laughter and tears, dreams and fears, with an unbreakable bond. I remember the sound of her laughter echoing through our home, the warmth of her embrace as she enveloped me in a hug when I got home from school and the light in her eyes as she gazed up at me with unconditional love. In her, I found a sense of purpose. It was a reason to find happiness even when the world seemed hard and cold. I would tap her chest and the sound it made was a tangible representation of our bond and love.

Suddenly, I had someone to hug, someone to hold, someone to kiss and she reciprocated with equal fervour. She would cling to me like a baby koala to its mother. In many ways, I became her surrogate mother, nurturing and caring for her as if she were my own. As I look back on those precious years with Lily by my side, I am filled with gratitude for the gift of her presence in my life. She taught me what it means to love and be loved in return, to find strength in vulnerability, and to hold onto hope even in the darkest of times. In the embrace of her unconditional love, I found love, healing, and the courage in time to persist in reclaiming my voice and to speak my truth. And for that, I will be forever grateful to the baby sister who changed my life in ways I never could have imagined.

We loved to pretend together. Imaginative play has a unique impact on the development of children, especially for those who may experience dissociation or detachment from reality. For me, it became a lifeline. It was a way to escape the harsh realities of my world and find calm in a realm of make-believe. One vivid memory that stands out is the countless hours my siblings and I spent playing "mum and dad" in our father's little Morris Minor parked in front of the house in Havelock North, New Zealand. I was about 13 years old, but in our imaginative world, I was the Mum in the front seat, and Owen, who sat beside me in the in the passenger seat was Dad. Along the back seat was Lily, Jenny and our younger brother who played the role of our children. In the confined space of that car, we created an entire universe. It was a world where we were a loving family, embarking on imaginary adventures together. As we drove along, pretending to run errands or go on family outings, the boundaries between reality and fantasy blurred, and for a fleeting moment, we were free from the weight of our troubles.

Our imaginative play extended far beyond the confines of the car. In the sanctuary of our backyard, at whatever house we were living at, we transformed into anything our imaginations wanted us to be. We were proprietors of a bustling fish and chip shop, complete with makeshift menus, imaginary customers, and the tantalizing aroma of fried seafood wafting through the air. We drove trucks and airplanes. We were mermaids and astronauts. In those moments of play, we were able to shed the burdens of our daily lives and immerse ourselves in a world of endless possibilities. It was a form of therapy, a way to cope with the challenges we faced and find joy in the simple act of pretending and play. We were trying to find a world where we belonged.

I can still clearly remember those nights when Lily first came to live with us. Trying to get to sleep was nearly impossible because she just cried and cried. Every night, without fail, her wails would echo through the house. I remember one night, lying in bed and feeling so frustrated and heartbroken, that I said out loud, "She needs to be returned." Even at ten years old, I somehow knew deep down that it wasn't right for her to be away from her biological mother.

Lily's cries were more than just a baby's cries; they were filled with a primal longing, a yearning for the bond she had lost. It was like she was calling out for her mum, her soul desperate to reconnect with the one who had given her life. This was the primal wound at work, the deep, innate pain that comes from being separated from one's biological roots. For those two or three weeks, every night was the same. Lily's sobs filled the house, a constant reminder that she wasn't where she was meant to be.

Her soul was yearning, calling out into the night, and each cry seemed to pierce through the walls of our home and straight into my heart. I felt this overwhelming sadness and helplessness, thinking she needs to go home. I knew, even at that young age, that her tears were not just about being uncomfortable or scared in a new place. They were about something much deeper, a loss and longing that only her biological mother could soothe.

Every night, as I lay there listening to her, I felt a mix of sadness and a strange kind of wisdom, understanding that what Lily needed was beyond anything we could give her. She was mourning the loss of the primal connection she had with her mum, a wound that was raw and aching. And in my heart, I knew that the only thing that could truly comfort her was being back with her.

The concept of the primal wound is one that resonates deeply with many individuals who have experienced early separation from their biological mothers. It's a wound that begins at birth, or even before, when the essential bond between mother and child is severed, leaving behind a sense of loss and emptiness. For me, the primal wound was

Chapter 3   Lily

something I grappled with from the moment I entered this world. Being adopted at birth meant that I was separated from my biological mother, unable to form the secure attachment that is crucial for healthy development. Instead, I was thrust into a world where my needs went unmet, where I had to navigate the complexities of survival on my own.

Nancy Verrier's book, "The Primal Wound," became a Bible of sorts for many adoptees, offering validation for the deep-seated pain they felt but couldn't always articulate. It spoke to the emptiness, the isolation, and the longing for something that was lost before we even had the chance to know it. But the primal wound isn't exclusive to adoptees. It can occur in any situation where the attachment between mother and child is disrupted, whether it's due to adoption, foster care, or even medical interventions like prolonged stays in incubators. The absence of that secure attachment leaves a lasting imprint on the psyche, shaping the way we view ourselves and the world around us.

As I grew older, I became acutely aware of the ways in which the primal wound manifested in my life. I struggled with feelings of inadequacy, of never quite fitting in, of constantly seeking validation and acceptance from others. I had constructed a false self and a facade that I presented to the world in hopes of being loved and accepted. But beneath the surface, there was a deep-seated emptiness, a longing for something I couldn't quite name.

It wasn't until I began healing at 36 years old that I began to confront the primal wound head-on. Through counselling and self-reflection, I learned to peel back the layers of my false self and reconnect with my authentic self that had been buried beneath years of pain and longing. When we consider the primal wound, we're transported back to the very beginning of our existence—the womb. It's a time of connection, of intimacy, and of bonding between mother and child. Yet, for adoptees, this crucial bond is severed prematurely, leaving behind a void that echoes throughout our lives.

In my quest for finding the true me, I've left no stone unturned. I've delved deep into the recesses of my psyche, confronting the pain and longing that stem from this primal wound. And in my exploration, I've undertaken exercises that some might consider unconventional, including physical rebirth experiences. Through these exercises, I've sought to retrace the steps of my own birth, to experience the sensation of being held, of passing through the birthing canal and of entering the world anew. It's a process that may seem abstract to some, but for me, it has been an essential part of my healing.

By revisiting my own birth, I tapped into the primal emotions and sensations that came with being separated from my biological mother. Through guided visualisation and rebirthing breathwork, I let myself truly feel the depth of that loss and mourn the connection that was cut short before it even had a chance to form. I expressed these emotions through physical movements and vocal release, letting go of years of pent-up tension.

Afterwards, I took part in rituals and affirmations to mark my symbolic rebirth. I created a small ceremony for myself, lighting candles and speaking words of affirmation and self-love. Each word felt like a balm to my soul, a step towards healing the deep wound of separation. This led to emotional healing, self-awareness, and a renewed sense of purpose, helping me to embrace my true self. It was like peeling back layers of an onion, revealing the core of who I am and understanding how the trauma of my early separation had shaped me.

By revisiting my birth in this way, I tapped into those raw emotions and sensations from the moment I was separated from my biological mother. I allowed myself to feel the depth of that loss and mourn the severed connection. This wasn't just an emotional exercise; it was a deep, visceral experience that connected me to my earliest self on the most basic level. I've also discovered a sense of resilience and strength within myself. I've come to realize that while the wound may never fully heal, I have the power to transform my relationship with it—to embrace it as a part of my story, rather than allowing it to define me. Healing from adoption trauma often entails confronting not just the primal wound of separation at birth, but also the deep-seated mother wound that lingers within. It's a process that requires both introspection and empathy, as we seek to understand the complexities of our relationship with our mothers.

When I reflect on my own experience of the primal wound, I'm filled with gratitude and compassion for the woman who carried me in her womb. Despite the challenges she may have faced, she made the courageous decision to give me life. And for that, I am endlessly grateful. Yet, alongside this gratitude, there was also pain born from the sense of abandonment and rejection that often accompanies the adoptee experience. As a child, I grappled with feelings of unworthiness, of not being enough, of longing for a connection that felt perpetually out of reach. I've come to recognize that the primal wound runs deeper than mere abandonment. It's a wound rooted in the very fabric of our existence. The primal bond between mother and child was disrupted before it ever had the chance to fully form.

Through various modalities of healing, over decades, from kinesiology, inner child work, psychotherapy to deep introspection, I've begun to unravel the layers of pain and trauma that have shaped my relationship with my mothers. I've delved into the depths of my own psyche, confronting the feelings of inadequacy and longing that have long plagued me. And in doing so, I've discovered a newfound sense of empathy and understanding for my adopted mother's own struggles and pain. I've come to realize that her inability to provide the love and support I needed was not a reflection of her worth as a person, but rather a consequence of her own circumstances and limitations.

The primal wound is a complex and deeply ingrained aspect of the adoptee experience, characterized by the absence or conditional nature of maternal love. It's a wound that leaves lasting scars, shaping the way we perceive ourselves and our relationships with others. In my work as a counsellor, I've encountered countless individuals who carry the burden of this primal wound. For many, it's a wound that stems from a childhood marked by conditional love, where affection was withheld unless certain conditions were met. Good grades, tidy rooms and obedient behaviour became the currency through which love and validation were earned. I know this all too well from personal experience. My own adopted mother, despite her best intentions, struggled to offer the unconditional love and support that I so desperately needed. Instead, her love was often contingent upon my compliance with her expectations and standards.

I remember vividly the pain of her silent treatment as a pre-teen. The icy silence that would descend upon our home for days on end whenever I failed to meet her expectations was a form of emotional manipulation that left me feeling rejected and unworthy, as though my very existence was a disappointment to her. Was my mother jealous of me, as some have suggested? Jealous of my vibrancy and love for life, of my desire to go out with friends? Could it be that my mother was punishing me for my individualisation, for my growing independence and less blinded adoration, reverence, and reliance on her? Did my self-assurance trigger her own primal wounds of rejection from her mother? She controlled the narrative by cutting me off first.

It's a question I've pondered over the years, searching for

answers in the depths of my own psyche. What I've come to realise is that the root of her behaviour lies not in jealousy, but in her own unresolved wounds and insecurities. Perhaps she saw in me a spirit and resilience that she lacked. I have always had a brightness that shone even in the darkest of times. And perhaps, in her own way, she sought to dim that light, to mould me into someone more palatable to her own expectations.

As I grew older, I began to see my mother not just as a source of pain, but as a person shaped by her own experiences and traumas. She was a woman carrying the weight of her past, her own dreams unfulfilled, and her own heartaches unresolved. Her silent treatments were not about me, but about her struggle to cope with her own emotions and the life she found herself in. Despite the hurt, I found myself wanting to understand her, to bridge the gap between us. It wasn't easy. The silent treatments had built walls of resentment and misunderstanding. But slowly, I began to see glimpses of her vulnerability, moments where her guard was down, and I could see the woman beneath the façade. I saw her struggles, her fears, and her own unspoken pain.

But as an adoptee, this conditional love cut deeper than I could have ever imagined. It reinforced the feelings of abandonment and rejection that had haunted me since infancy, leaving me with a fear of being unlovable and unworthy of love. And it was through this process of healing that I discovered the transformative power of unconditional love and acceptance. In the safety of the counselling room, I found a space where I could be seen, heard, and validated for who I truly was. I created a space where I could begin to heal the wounds of the past and embrace the possibilities of the future.

Today, as a coach and counsellor myself, I strive to create that same safe space for others who are grappling with their own wounds. I know firsthand the impact that a nurturing and validating environment can have on the healing process, and I am committed to walking alongside my clients as they find their own way towards wholeness and self-discovery. The wounds may never fully disappear, but through compassion, understanding, and the power of human connection, we can learn to heal and thrive in spite of it. And in doing so, we reclaim our birthright to live authentically and embrace the fullness of who we are.

Healing in Practice

Engaging in play and imaginative play, even as an adult, can have numerous therapeutic and psychological benefits:

- Stress Relief: Imaginative play allows adults to take a break from the pressures and responsibilities of daily life, providing a much-needed mental escape and reducing stress.
- Creativity and Innovation: Engaging in imaginative play can stimulate creativity and problem-solving skills, helping adults think outside the box and come

up with innovative solutions in their personal and professional lives.

- Improved Relationships: Shared imaginative play can strengthen bonds and improve communication with others, fostering a sense of connection and empathy.
- Joy and Fulfillment: Imaginative play brings a sense of joy and fulfillment, reminding adults of the simple pleasures in life and enhancing overall well-being.
- Self-Discovery: Through play, adults can reconnect with their inner child, rediscovering passions, interests, and aspects of their personality that may have been suppressed or forgotten.
- Resilience Building: Imaginative play can build resilience by allowing adults to experiment with different roles and outcomes, helping them develop coping strategies and a more positive outlook on life.

Incorporating imaginative play into your adult life can be a powerful tool for maintaining mental health, fostering creativity, and enhancing emotional well-being.

Examples from themed parties, interactive theatre, creative writing circles, board games, outdoor sports, dance classes and camping trips

Self-Assessment Questions

How have feelings of inadequacy or the need for validation influenced the way you presented yourself to others?

What steps have you taken to peel back the layers of your false self and reconnect with your authentic self?

Describe an activity or type of play that provided you with relief or joy during tough times. Reflect on how this helped you handle your environment and what lasting impact it had on you.

Chapter 4

Growing Up

Growing up as an adopted kid, I struggled not just with the lack of biological connections but with a massive identity crisis. Without siblings, parents, family friends, relatives, or familiar faces that mirrored my own, I went through adolescence feeling deeply isolated. School was like a battleground where I fought hard to hide the inner turmoil that threatened to swallow me whole. I slapped on a happy face, trying to mask the pain and loneliness that gnawed at me. But underneath that cheerful exterior, I felt a strong sense of disconnection from the world around me. No one knew the depths of my suffering or the silent battles I fought within my own mind. I desperately wanted someone to see through the facade, to recognise the pain lurking beneath the surface. In a world where appearances were everything, my inner turmoil stayed hidden. Behind a bright and sunny mask, a silent scream echoed from the depths of my soul.

Around the age of thirteen, however, a shift occurred within me. It was as if a switch had been flipped, unleashing a flood of worries and insecurities that never seemed to ebb. Fear became a constant companion, whispering doubts into the recesses of my mind. I was a timid, low self-esteem girl, plagued by a sense of inadequacy that seemed to overshadow everything else. My body, once small and fragile, began to feel like a burden, its slow development a source of shame and embarrassment. While my peers blossomed into their teenage years, I lagged behind, a late bloomer in every sense of the word.

At school, I watched as my friends grew taller, developed curves, and started experimenting with makeup and fashion. Meanwhile, I remained stuck in a childlike body, feeling awkward and out of place. PE classes were a nightmare, where changing in front of the other girls only highlighted my lack of development. I dreaded social events and avoided situations where my insecurities might be exposed.

I remember one particular incident at a school dance when I overheard a group of girls giggling about how I looked. Their words cut deep, reinforcing the belief that I was different, and not in a good way. I felt like an outsider, not just within my adoptive family, but in every social circle I tried to be part of.

At home, things weren't much better. My adoptive parents, though well-meaning, didn't quite understand the depth of my struggles. They offered reassurances, telling me I'd catch up eventually, but their words felt hollow. The primal wound of being separated from my biological mother festered, manifesting as a constant ache that I couldn't shake.

In those moments of deep insecurity, I would retreat to my room, seeking solace in books and daydreams. Stories became my escape, a way to forget about my own life and lose myself in the adventures of fictional characters who seemed to have it all together. I longed for the confidence and ease they displayed, wishing I could magically transform into someone else, someone more confident and less plagued by doubts.

It was during one particularly mundane school holiday, just on the cusp of my teenage years, that I stumbled upon a place that would change the course of my life forever. I had never really looked forward to school holidays, finding them suffocating in the crowded confines of our small home. So, on that fateful day, I made a decision that would alter my trajectory in ways I couldn't have imagined.

Skipping the final afternoon of school, I walked away down the familiar road that led away from the noise and chaos of my everyday existence. With each step, I felt a sense of liberation wash over me, a freedom born from the simple act of defying what was expected of me. Eventually, my aimless wandering led me to a garden centre, its entrance adorned with vibrant blooms and lush greenery. Without hesitation, I approached the counter and, with a courage I didn't know I possessed, asked for a job.

The woman behind the counter looked at me with a mix of surprise and amusement. She was middle-aged, with kind eyes and a warm smile. "Do you have any experience with plants?" she asked, her tone more curious than sceptical.

"Not really," I admitted, "but I'm a keen learner and I'm willing to do whatever it takes."

Chapter 4   Growing Up

She studied me for a moment, perhaps sensing the desperation and determination in my voice. "Well, we could use some extra hands around here, especially with spring coming up. How about you start with some basic tasks and we'll see how it goes?"

From the moment I set foot in Dean's Garden Way, I knew I had found my sanctuary. Surrounded by the soothing embrace of nature, I felt a sense of belonging that had eluded me for so long. Weekends and school holidays became synonymous with the rhythmic hum of life within the garden I tended to the plants with a care and devotion that bordered on reverence, finding purpose and peace in the quiet companionship. Each morning, I arrived early, breathing in the crisp, dewy air and greeting the flowers as if they were old friends. The garden centre became my sanctuary, a place where I could lose myself in the simple, soothing rhythms of nature.

There was something healing about the routine. Watering the plants, pruning the leaves, and watching them grow instilled a sense of calm and accomplishment that I hadn't felt in years. The vibrant colours and delicate petals were a constant reminder of life's beauty and resilience.

One day, my boss noticed my dedication and offered to teach me more advanced gardening techniques. She showed me how to propagate cuttings, mix soil for different types of plants, and even how to recognise and treat common plant diseases. Her patience and knowledge were invaluable, and I soaked up every bit of information she shared.

"You've got a real knack for this," she said one afternoon, as we worked side by side repotting a series of small ferns. "Have you thought about pursuing horticulture more seriously?"

The idea had never occurred to me before. Gardening had been a refuge, a way to escape the chaos of my life, but as she spoke, I began to see it as something more—a potential future, a career path that I could genuinely be passionate about.

"I'd love to," I admitted, feeling a spark of excitement at the thought. "I never really knew what I wanted to do, but this… this feels right."

When I was 14, I came home from Rangers (Girl Guides) to find I had another new baby brother, the tenth child to join our family. Instead of feeling joy, I was overwhelmed. I often wondered why my parents felt the need to keep growing our already large family. With each new little one, the load seemed to get heavier, and the strain on our family's resources became more noticeable, making things feel a bit more stretched than they already were.

It wasn't just the financial strain that weighed heavily on us, but the emotional toll of caring for children with mental health problems and behavioural issues. Our parents, ill-equipped to handle the complexities of our individual struggles, often found themselves overwhelmed by the sheer magnitude of our needs. I can't help but wonder how different things might have been if someone had intervened or if a social worker had knocked on our door and peered beneath the surface of our seemingly chaotic household. But the truth is, no one ever did.

Chapter 4   Growing Up

Our family's struggles remained hidden behind closed doors, shielded from prying eyes by a veil of silence and shame.

As a child, I felt like a ghost, drifting through life without a voice to call my own. Dissociation became my refuge, a coping mechanism to numb the pain and disconnect from the chaos that surrounded me. I retreated into myself, cocooned in a shell of stoic silence and solitude, unable to articulate the turmoil that raged within.

Growing up in a mixed-race adopted household was marked by neglect and emotional complexities that often felt overwhelming. As a teenager, the desire to fit in burned within me like a relentless fire, yet the reality of my family's composition seemed to cast a shadow over my attempts to blend seamlessly into the fabric of society. I vividly remember many times I felt the sting of embarrassment and shame at the sight of my unconventional family. Surrounded by siblings of varying races—white, brown, black—I couldn't help but feel like an outsider in my own home. The disapproving stares of strangers and the whispered comments behind our backs only served to deepen the sense of inadequacy that gnawed at my soul.

I longed to be like everyone else, to belong to a family that looked and acted the way families were supposed to. But instead, I found myself grappling with the harsh reality of our unconventional existence, a reality that seemed to defy societal norms at every turn. There was no other option but for me to retreat into my own fantasy world. For years, I lived in a state of numbness, disconnected from my body and my emotions. All I knew was that I didn't like it and that something inside me felt broken and irreparable. I was a messed-up cookie, a casualty of circumstances beyond my control.

As a therapist, I have encountered countless individuals who grapple with the disconnection from their own bodies and emotions, seeking refuge in the safety of their inner worlds. Treating dissociation requires a delicate balance of compassion and understanding and a recognition that the journey towards healing is a deeply personal and often painful one. In my practice, I approach each client with the utmost gentleness, creating a space where they can begin to explore the depths of their experiences without fear of judgment or criticism.

The therapeutic relationship serves as a lifeline for many individuals, offering a rare opportunity to experience unconditional true connection and acceptance for the first time. It is a place where they can slowly begin to unravel the layers of numbness and disconnection that have shielded them from the harsh realities of their past.

For many people including adopted individuals, dissociation becomes a way of life. It is a means of escaping the overwhelming emotions and uncertainties that accompany their unique upbringing. From a young age, they learn to retreat into a world of fantasy and imagination, seeking respite in the familiar embrace of Dreamland.

But while dissociation may offer temporary relief from the pain, it also serves to perpetuate a cycle of avoidance and detachment. In therapy, we work together to gently coax them out of their inner sanctuaries, guiding them toward a deeper understanding of themselves and their experiences. It is a gradual process, marked by moments of resistance and breakthroughs, but with patience and perseverance, many individuals begin to reclaim their sense of self. They learn to confront the shame and embarrassment that have long plagued them, finding the courage to face reality head-on. My role is not to rush the process or force them to confront their demons before they are ready. Instead, I provide a safe and supportive environment where they can explore their innermost thoughts and feelings at their own pace.

Cross country running became another sanctuary, a place where I could escape the noise of my crowded household and lose myself in the simple act of putting one foot in front of the other. It was a form of mindfulness, though I didn't realize it at the time and a way to connect with my body and quiet the incessant chatter of my mind. There were no chauffeured rides to sports practices or any other extracurricular activities. It was just me, my running shoes, and the open road. But running was more than just a form of exercise; it was a connection to my dad, a rare moment of one-on-one time in a family where such moments were few and far between. As I pounded the pavement, my dad would ride alongside me on his motorised scooter, offering words of encouragement and support.

In the solitude of those long runs, I discovered something. I found a resilience and determination that had been lying dormant within me all along. With each mile, I found strength in my own footsteps, a connection with my body and a reminder that even in the face of adversity, I was capable of forging my own path forward. And though my running may have begun as a means of escape, it has evolved into something far more. It became a testament to the power of perseverance and emotional and physical resilience I had within me.

In those fleeting moments on the open road, I felt a bond with my dad that transcended the constraints of our everyday lives. It was a gift and one that I cherished deeply, even if it didn't happen as often as I would have liked. Growing up in a large family meant learning to fend for myself, and I needed to find support elsewhere in unconventional places like running and the garden centre.

Running became my escape, a way to clear my mind and feel a sense of freedom that was often missing from my daily routine. I'd lace up my shoes and take to the trails, finding solace in the rhythm of my footsteps and the rush of wind against my face. Each stride was a step away from the chaos at home and a step toward my own sense of peace and autonomy. I didn't realise how much I relied on it until we would head off on holidays.

With no funds for extravagant trips and no time for elaborate outings, we relied on the simplicity of Dad's Kingswood—a sturdy station wagon that took us everywhere we couldn't walk to. Living near schools meant that walking was our primary mode of transportation, a practical necessity in a household overflowing with children. But when it came time for family holidays, the Kingswood carried us to destinations both near and far. From farm stays to beach getaways, each trip was an adventure in its own right. It was a chance to escape the confines of our everyday lives and explore new horizons together.

I can still vividly recall the chaotic scene as we piled into the car, luggage stacked precariously on the roof, and children crammed into every available space. Dad would take the wheel, navigating the winding roads with practiced ease, while we kids jostled for position in the backseat. Yet, beneath the surface of our idyllic family vacations, there lurked an undercurrent of tension and discord. My sibling who struggled with a myriad of behavioural issues, often cast a shadow over our outings with disruptive tantrums and outbursts. For me and Owen the boot of the Kingswood became our designated spot. It was a cramped but cozy nook where we could gaze out at the passing scenery and a strange juxtaposition, facing outward while the world whizzed by in a blur of motion. It could be a metaphor, perhaps, for the disjointed nature of our family life.

As we left, a wave of fear would wash over me. For me, vacations were not a time of relaxation and enjoyment, but rather a source of deep-seated anxiety and unease. I longed for the safety and familiarity of home, where my garden and my bed were safe and known. Growing up as an adopted child, I felt fear and unsafe often. I had a sense of loss and disconnection that stemmed from the separation from my biological mother. Though I may not have understood it at the time, this primal wound lay at the root of my fears and anxieties, rearing its head whenever I found myself in unfamiliar territory. On holidays, the primal wound would rear its head, triggering a cascade of fear and panic that threatened to overwhelm me. It wasn't a conscious choice to act out or cause trouble. To be inpatient, short and rude and disagree with my siblings and parents. It was a desperate attempt to regain a sense of control in a world that felt increasingly unfamiliar and unsafe. My days and weeks were so controlled and planned so to go on a holiday I felt scared and nervous.

Looking back, I can see now that my behaviour was not a reflection of who I truly was, but rather a manifestation of the deep-seated anxiety that gripped me from within. It was a plea for someone to recognize the pain and turmoil that lay beneath the surface. And though those family holidays may have been tinged with fear and uncertainty, they were also a reminder of the resilience that lay within me. For even in the darkest moments, I found the strength to face my fears head-on.

I realize now that trauma is a universal experience. It is a thread that binds us all together in the tapestry of human existence. But what sets us apart is how we choose to navigate that trauma, how we allow it to shape our identities and define our relationships. For me, living with a survival personality became a coping mechanism born from the deep-seated need to be loved and accepted. From a young age, I learned to adapt and mould myself to fit the expectations of others, sacrificing my own authenticity in the process, sacrificing my own needs to tend to theirs in the hope they would accept me.

But what exactly is a survival personality? It's the mask we wear to shield ourselves from the pain of rejection and abandonment and a false self-crafted from a desire for love and validation. It's the person we become when we believe that our worth is contingent upon the approval of others. Growing up in a household where love and acceptance were often scarce commodities, I learned to become a master chameleon, shifting and morphing to meet the ever-changing demands of my environment. Whether it meant mimicking the quiet introversion of my parents or suppressing my own conflicting desires, I was willing to do whatever it took to earn a slither of affection.

But this chameleon type behaviour came at a cost. I suffered a loss of self and a deep-seated sense of confusion and disconnection. I had become so adept at wearing masks and playing roles that I had lost sight of who I truly was beneath the layers of pretence. Desperation clung to me like a heavy haze, weaving its tendrils through the fabric of my existence. From the depths of my soul, I yearned for a love that seemed forever elusive, just out of reach like a distant star in the night sky above the fog.

Smothering my longing for love and light was a growing darkness. It was a shadow cast over my childhood, poisoning the wellspring of affection and connection that I so desperately craved. It came in the form of my mother's growing cruelty that cut me to the core and left me reeling in its wake. I can still feel the sting of her rejection, like a knife twisting in my heart. It was the strongest when I was fourteen, a time when I was beginning to find my voice and forge connections with others outside of our insular family unit. But to my mother, these budding friendships were a threat—a reminder of the love and acceptance that she could not—or would not—provide.

Her weapon of choice was silence. Her icy silence might stretch on for days, leaving me living constantly on edge. For an adoptee, this was one of the cruellest forms of punishment imaginable and a rejection that cut to the very core of my identity. I can still remember the feeling, like cold water cascading over me, an unwelcome reminder of my mother's disapproval. It was her way of putting me back in my box and of reminding me of my place in the pecking order of her affections. And though I tried desperately to please her, to earn a scrap of love or approval, it was never enough.

My whole life became a dedicated dance of seeking validation from a mother who seemed incapable of giving it. I moulded myself into the perfect daughter, bending and contorting to fit the ever-shifting contours of her expectations. But no matter how hard I tried, there was no love, only emptiness and longing. From a young age, I learned to read my mother's energy like a seasoned detective, attuned to the subtle shifts in her mood and demeanour. It wasn't a gift, as I once believed, but rather a trauma response—a desperate attempt to gauge how much of myself I could reveal without risking her rejection.

I've seen it time and time again in my work as a coach and counsellor. Those who have experienced the security of a secure attachment with their adoptive parents and biological parents are better equipped to navigate the challenges of life. But for those who have been denied that fundamental sense of belonging, the road ahead is fraught with peril. I often bear witness to the struggles of those who have lost touch with their own identities, their sense of self eroded by a lifetime of seeking validation and approval from others. For many, the fear of rejection looms large, a constant shadow that threatens to engulf them in a never-ending cycle of self-doubt and self-rejection. But what lies at the heart of this desperate quest for love and acceptance? It's a question that I ponder as I sit across from my clients, watching as they unravel the tangled web of their own insecurities and fears.

In a world where so many of us are conditioned to seek love and acceptance outside of ourselves, the way to authenticity is a radical act of self-liberation. It's a reclaiming of our true essence, a celebration of our inherent worthiness, and a testament to the power of self-love to transform our lives. And while the path may be challenging, the rewards are immeasurable—a life lived authentically, in alignment with our deepest truths is inner wealth.

A person who was never given the opportunity to discover their authentic self was Owen. Always just left of centre of our tumultuous family dynamics, he was a quiet, introverted soul who found an escape in the realms of Dungeons and Dragons. But while his passion for the game provided an escape from the control and chaos of our household, it also brought him into direct conflict with our parents.

My parents didn't understand Owen. They didn't understand his love for fantasy worlds and imaginary quests. To them, he was simply an "inside kid" and a loner who preferred the confines of his own imagination to the bustling world outside. And yet, Owen was so much more than that. He was a complex individual, caught between the worlds of introversion and extroversion, longing for connection yet hesitant to venture beyond the safety of his own thoughts. Cleanliness and social graces were of little concern to him, his mind consumed by the intricacies of the games he loved.

But what my parents failed to realize was that Owen's struggles ran deeper than they could ever imagine. As an adoptee himself, he grappled with a sense of identity and belonging that eluded him at every turn. And in a family that failed to understand or accept him for who he truly was, his sense of rejection only grew deeper. In the hustle and bustle of our crowded household, Owen and I often found ourselves in the background, overshadowed by the needs of our younger siblings. Yet, amidst the chaos, we forged a bond, spending evenings watching on television "MASH" together, a small reprieve from the whirlwind around us.

Despite the challenges we faced, there was something

strong within me. It was a quiet resilience that refused to be dimmed. While Owen grappled with feelings of inadequacy and silence, I possessed an unwavering determination, a fierce spirit that seemed to drive me forward. From a young age, I observed this innate drive within myself, a relentless pursuit of goals, achieving and aspirations. While I set my sights on academic achievements (which did not come easily to me) and career paths, Owen wasn't one for setting concrete goals or chasing academic accolades. Instead, he found safety and structure in the simplicity of everyday tasks, finding joy in the quiet moments of life.

But beneath his stoic exterior lay a deep well of sadness, a longing for something more that he couldn't quite articulate. As the years passed and I approached the threshold of adulthood, Dean's Garden Way became more than just a place of employment. It became a refuge, a haven where I could shed the weight of expectations and simply be myself. In the nurturing embrace of the natural world, I discovered facets of myself that had long lain dormant, buried beneath layers of insecurity and self-doubt. With each passing day, I felt a little more seen, a little more understood. I was able to be loud, silly, belly laugh, talk too much and share about my future plans and the hardship at home. Having introverted quiet parents, I felt I needed to be like them to be accepted. By the time I left for university at eighteen, I was no longer the timid, withdrawn girl who had first walked through the doors of Dean's Garden Way. I was someone who had been seen, loved, and accepted for exactly who I was. My own blossoming was a testament to the transformative power of nature and the healing balm of unconditional acceptance from my wok colleagues and the couple of girlfriends who joined me in my garden centre days.

As I embarked on the next chapter of my life at university, Dean's Garden Way bid me farewell in a way that touched the deepest corners of my heart. They orchestrated a clandestine going-away party, a gesture of love and appreciation that left me speechless. Secretive drop-offs, heartfelt celebrations, and thoughtful gifts marked the occasion, reaffirming the bond I had forged with my surrogate family. Their kindness and support meant more to me than they could ever know, especially amidst the turmoil that raged within the walls of my own home. My older sister battle with mental health and my deaf sister's behavioural issues cast a shadow over our household, adding yet another layer of complexity to an already tumultuous upbringing.

In hindsight, it's clear that my connection to nature was more than just a hobby or a job. It was a lifeline, a tether to the world that kept me grounded when everything else seemed uncertain. And as I reflect on my life, I can't help but wonder if it was this deep connection to the earth that ultimately sustained me, even in my darkest moments. For me, nature wasn't just a place to escape. It was a place to belong. And in a world where acceptance was often hard to come by, I found peace in the beauty of the natural world, a reminder that even in the depths of despair, there is always something worth holding on to. Owen didn't have that. He never felt tethered to the earth, so he simply let go.

Healing in Practice

At its core, the desire to please others at any cost is a form of self-rejection and a betrayal of the very essence of who we are. In our relentless pursuit of love and approval, we lose sight of ourselves, sacrificing our own needs and desires on the altar of someone else's happiness. But the irony is that in our quest to avoid rejection from others, we ultimately end up becoming disappointed, disconnected from ourselves and rejecting ourselves. We silence our own voices, suppress our own needs, and deny ourselves the love and compassion that we so desperately crave. It is this very lack of identity that leaves us vulnerable to the darkest depths of despair. For when we lose sight of who we are, we lose touch with the inherent worth and value that lies within us. We become adrift in a sea of self-hatred and self-doubt, disconnected from the very essence of our humanity.

These emotional states can trigger chronic inflammation, IBS, elevated cortisol levels, migraines, gut issues, food intolerances, and insomnia. Stress disrupts the gut-brain axis and immune response, leading to a host of physical ailments. High cortisol affects sleep and metabolism, while chronic stress imbalances the autonomic nervous system. These symptoms highlight the deep connection between mind and body, emphasizing the importance of self-care, support, and finding purpose. Healing requires addressing both emotional and physiological aspects, reminding us to nurture our whole being with compassion and intention.

For those who are able to reclaim their sense of self, there is a path forward toward healing and wholeness. It begins with reconnecting with the tender parts of ourselves, with embracing our own vulnerabilities and imperfections. It requires us to slow down, to listen to the whispers of our own hearts, and to hold ourselves with the same love and compassion that we so freely offer to others.

I have seen firsthand the devastating toll that this loss of identity can take. It's a slow spiral downward, marked by feelings of hopelessness, despair and disconnect from the very things that make life worth living: love, kindness, and compassion.

Enormous suffering. Unbearable pain. These are the shadows that lurk in the corners of our minds, the silent burdens we carry with us each day. But how do we navigate the depths of our own pain when there's no one to turn to, no one to reach out to and say, "I'm in pain"? As a teenager, triggers seemed to lurk around every corner, waiting to pounce when I least expected it.

One of the biggest triggers for me was my own inner critic. In my mind, there was a relentless voice that compared my body to those of my peers. While other girls were blossoming into womanhood, I felt stuck in a perpetual state of immaturity, unable to keep pace with the changes unfolding around me. It was a source of deep shame and insecurity, leaving me feeling inadequate and unworthy.

But triggers weren't limited to my physical appearance. They extended to my interactions with others as well. Anytime I felt excluded or overlooked, whether it be within my family or among friends, I was overwhelmed by sadness and a feeling of isolation. It was as if I didn't belong anywhere, as if I were somehow defective or damaged beyond repair. I craved connection and companionship, yet I couldn't bear the thought of being alone with my own thoughts. I wasn't equipped to discover and become my authentic self.

The transformation from the false self to the authentic self is one of the most important transformations a person can undergo. The false self is the persona we construct to navigate the world, often shaped by early experiences and conditioned responses to our environment. It's the mask we wear to seek approval and love from others, born out of a deep-seated fear of rejection. This false self is adaptive, but ultimately, it's not who we truly are.

In contrast, the authentic self is the essence of our being, untainted by external influences. It's the core of our identity, grounded in self-love and acceptance. Unlike the false self, the authentic self doesn't seek validation from external sources. Instead, it draws from an internal wellspring of love and compassion, embracing both our strengths and vulnerabilities.

The path to authenticity begins with inner healing and self-awareness. Through therapy, coaching and introspection, individuals can unravel the layers of conditioning that have shaped their false self, confronting unresolved trauma and challenging ingrained beliefs. Therapeutic techniques such as inner child work, reparenting and mindfulness-based interventions can help individuals cultivate self-awareness and develop healthier patterns of thinking and behaviour. By learning to identify and challenge negative thought patterns, individuals can begin to dismantle the walls of their false self, paving the way for the emergence of their authentic self.

However, the way to authenticity is not easy. It requires courage, vulnerability, and a willingness to confront the parts of ourselves we may have long suppressed. For those who have lived in a state of numbness or dissociation, reconnecting with their emotions can be an unbearable prospect. Yet, it's through this process of feeling and healing that true transformation occurs. Ultimately, the key to unlocking the authentic self lies in cultivating a deep, loving relationship with oneself. This means embracing all aspects of who we are—our strengths, weaknesses, joys, and sorrows—without judgment or self-rejection. It's about recognizing that our worthiness is inherent, not contingent upon external validation.

Self-Assessment Questions

Have you ever struggled with feelings of inadequacy and low self-esteem during your formative years? How did you come to accept and embrace your unique journey, and what helped you find confidence in yourself?

Chapter 4   Growing Up

Have you ever experienced a sense of isolation and disconnection during an identity crisis? How did you cope with the inner turmoil, and what steps did you take to find a sense of belonging and self-acceptance?

Have you ever felt a quiet resilience within you that helped you overcome challenges and pursue your goals? How has this inner drive shaped your path, especially in contrast to others around you who may have taken different approaches to finding joy and fulfillment?

Chapter 5

Leaving Home

As I hit my late teens, the idea of leaving home started to feel like a big deal. In our family, it was pretty much expected that you'd move out at 18. But just thinking about leaving Lily and my other siblings behind made me feel so guilty. Even though I knew it was time to get out there and start my own adventure, I couldn't shake a sense of abandonment for leaving them. That's when I really started to get just how deep our bond was.

Enrolling in a two-year diploma program in horticulture at Massey University in Palmerston North, with a year practical and a year academic, gave me a real sense of purpose and direction amidst the confusion of my inner life. Leaving behind the structured, controlled environment of my childhood felt like stepping into an unknown world where rules were scarce, and the weight of responsibility was heavy on my shoulders. I was filled with a mix of eagerness and nervousness.

The shift from the familiar routines and rules of home to the bustling hostel life was both exhilarating and overwhelming. In my newfound freedom, I found myself indulging in some pretty reckless behaviour, driven by a desire to break free from the constraints of my upbringing. Late-night parties, spontaneous road trips, and impromptu adventures became the norm. I was soaking up every bit of the freedom I'd craved for so long, but it was also a bit of a wild ride. Balancing my studies with this newfound lifestyle was tricky, but the thrill of exploring my own path kept me going.

Despite the chaos, my passion for horticulture remained my anchor. The hands-on work with plants and the deep dives into academic study provided a steadying force in my life. My coursework and practical experiences were fascinating, offering me a glimpse into a world I genuinely wanted to be a part of. While I was pushing boundaries and testing limits, I was also discovering who I was outside the rigid framework of my family's expectations. This period of my life was a crucial time of growth, filled with both mistakes and triumphs. It helped me understand that finding balance and carving out my own identity was a process, one that required patience, resilience, and a lot of learning along the way.

In those early months at university, I found comfort at the bottom of a glass. The numbness that alcohol provided was a temporary escape from the overwhelming emotions churning inside me. Without the familiar constraints of home, I felt adrift, lost in a sea of uncertainty and confusion. My behaviour was erratic, my decisions impulsive.

I'd ride through the streets on a little yellow motorised scooter called Melody, seeking refuge in the dimly lit corners of the local pub. The nights blurred together in a haze of alcohol-induced oblivion, and I revelled in the freedom to lose myself in the moment. Alcohol became my sanctuary, a way where I could hide from the weight of my responsibilities and quiet the noise inside my head.

Every night was an adventure, filled with spontaneous decisions and wild antics in the university hostel that was now home. I'd chat with my peers, party without a care, and let the booze wash away my worries. The hostel's familiar faces soon became my makeshift family, offering a sense of belonging that I hadn't felt in a long time. But as the initial thrill of this reckless freedom began to wear off, the reality of my choices started to sink in. The hangovers became harder to shake, and the nights of fun felt emptier. I realised that while I was trying to escape my problems, I was only creating new ones.

The abundance of food on campus served as a stark reminder of the privilege I now possessed. Surrounded by plenty, I struggled to find my place in a world where abundance only served to magnify my sense of emptiness. Beneath the surface, I was grappling with a sense of loneliness and isolation that I couldn't shake. Sharing a room with my roommate, my outward demeanour betrayed the inner turmoil I was experiencing. I buried my feelings deep, unwilling to confront the emptiness that gnawed at my soul.

She was a vibrant and happy person, always surrounded by friends and laughter. Her energy was infectious, but it also made me feel even more isolated. I envied her ease in social situations, the confidence she oozed and her ability to connect

Chapter 5   Leaving Home

with others effortlessly. In contrast, I felt like I was drowning in a sea of faces, unable to find a lifeline.

Each day, I put on a brave face, pretending to be just as carefree and happy as everyone else. But inside, I was a mess. The dining hall, with its endless buffet of options, became a battleground. Every meal was a reminder of the scarcity I had known growing up, and I found it difficult to reconcile this new reality with my past. I often ate alone, picking at my food, my appetite dulled by the weight of my thoughts.

Amidst the sea of unfamiliar faces, I found support in the company of a gentle young man in the same university studies as me. His quiet demeanour and gentle nature resonated with me, and I soon found myself harbouring feelings for him. We'd spend hours talking about everything and nothing, his calm presence providing a much-needed anchor in my chaotic world. My lack of experience in matters of the heart left me paralysed with indecision. I would overanalyse every interaction, second-guessing myself at every turn. Before I could muster the courage to confess my feelings, he had already found a girlfriend. I remember the moment vividly seeing them together for the first time felt like a punch to the gut and a feeling like I had been replaced. The heartbreak that followed served as a harsh reminder of my own naivety and innocence.

Despite my best efforts to navigate the complexities of relationships, I found myself ill-equipped to handle the tumultuous emotions that accompanied them. I would lie awake at night, replaying every conversation, wondering what I had done wrong or what I could have done differently. The pain of unrequited love and the jealousy that gnawed at me were new and overwhelming. His new relationship was a constant, painful reminder of my missed opportunity. I would see them together, laughing and sharing moments, and it felt like a spotlight on my inadequacies. I found myself withdrawing, avoiding places where I might run into them. My mind became a battleground, filled with overthinking, analysing, criticising, and worrying. Every interaction was dissected, every word spoken was scrutinised.

In an attempt to cope, I buried my feelings deep inside. I threw myself into what my future looked like and how I could make it happen, hoping to distract myself from the turmoil within. But no matter how busy I kept myself, the underlying sadness lingered and I found these emotions difficult. It wasn't an easy process, and there were many days when I felt like I was taking one step forward and two steps back. But gradually, I started to heal. I found solace in journaling, writing down my thoughts and feelings as a way to process them.

Another friendship at university would set the stage for a new chapter in my life, alongside another mentor figure who provided unwavering support and guidance throughout my academic career, my friendships would prove to be a beacon of light in the darkness. With my friend's encouragement, I found myself embarking on a new adventure, after graduating from university, one that would take me to working in a pub at Waikiki Beach filled with exhilaration and anxiety.

Chapter 5   Leaving Home

Arriving at Waikiki Beach, I was greeted by a world of unfamiliar sights and sounds. As I poured beers and navigated the intricacies of pub life, I found myself thrust into a whirlwind of new experiences. From my first introduction to marijuana to the clumsy attempts at pouring a perfect beer, each moment served as a lesson in humility and self-discovery.

As I approached adulthood, the urge to uncover the secrets of my past became more and more intense. I couldn't shake the feeling that there was something missing, something important that I needed to discover. So, I made a choice that I knew would change everything. I decided to search for my biological mother. I applied for my original birth certificate, eager to unearth the secrets it held. Yet, my excitement was short-lived as the document returned with a veto, shattering my dreams of discovering my true identity. I was forced to confront the harsh reality that I would have to wait until the age of 28 for the veto to be lifted. I was devastated and it felt like I couldn't wait that long.

I decided to listen to the inner calling and travel to Australia and then on to England to try and find my birth mother. And myself. Leaving New Zealand at 19 and 6 months was meant to be a moment of liberation, a step towards independence and self-discovery. Yet, as I reflect on that day, the overwhelming sense of guilt and sorrow still lingers, casting a shadow over the memories of departure.

It was a hectic morning, with my mother juggling the responsibilities of caring for my younger siblings while preparing to see me off. The bus to Auckland for the flight to Sydney, Australia awaited, marking the beginning of a new chapter in my life, but also signalling the end of an era. In that moment, I longed to express the depth of my emotions, to convey the sadness that threatened to consume me. But words failed me, stifled by the suffocating silence that permeated our family and a silence that spoke volumes about the emotional distance that existed between us. My mother, pressed for time, hurriedly bid me farewell, a fleeting hug serving as a final goodbye. In that moment, I felt the sting of abandonment and the abruptness of our parting left me reeling. It was as if a chapter of my life had ended abruptly, with no opportunity for closure or reflection.

The decision to leave wasn't easy. I spent countless nights agonising over the choice, torn between the desire to forge my own path and the responsibility I felt towards my siblings, especially Lily. Saying goodbye to her was the hardest part. I remember holding her tight, her small frame trembling against mine, both of us silently crying. Her big, questioning eyes seemed to ask why I had to leave, and the guilt of abandoning her weighed heavily on my heart. As the vehicle pulled away, my younger sister Jenny rode her bike alongside me, her blonde hair fluttered in the wind. Silent tears streamed down my face and my heart was heavy. It wasn't the farewell I was hoping for.

Over the years that followed, my departure haunted me. It was a constant source of anguish and regret. The infrequent

Chapter 5   Leaving Home

phone calls from my mother served as painful reminders of the chasm that had formed between us. In leaving home, I had hoped to find freedom and purpose, but instead, I found myself burdened by the weight of guilt and sorrow. It would take many years and countless moments of introspection to find peace with my decision, to reconcile the conflicting emotions that had plagued me for so long. But even now, as I look back on that day, the memories are tinged with a bittersweet sadness.

Arriving in Sydney marked the beginning of a new chapter in my life filled with uncertainty, adventure, and unexpected twists and turns. With my friend Donna by my side, I embarked on a journey that would take me across cities and landscapes, leading me to unexpected encounters and life-changing decisions. Initially, I stayed with my oldest brother in Sydney, seeking refuge in the warmth of family amidst the chaos of a bustling city. But as days turned into weeks, the confines of their unit became increasingly cramped, prompting Donna and me to seek out our own space.

We found a unit near the iconic Sydney Opera House, where I landed a job serving milkshakes and hamburgers at a nearby cafe. Despite my best efforts, I struggled to keep track of customer's orders, often leaving them frustrated and dissatisfied. But amidst the chaos of my newfound responsibilities, I found security in the camaraderie of my fellow employees and the vibrant energy of the city.

After a few months, Donna and I decided to embark on a trip across the Nullarbor, a vast expanse of land that stretched endlessly before us. The three-day bus ride brought us to Perth, where I found a job selling security systems during the day. I met Flick and Mick, fellow adventurers who shared my zest for life and thirst for new experiences. Together, we rented a house, creating a sanctuary amidst the uncertainty of our transient lives. In the depths of my confusing emotions and periods of despair, I turned to drugs to numb the pain. Marijuana became my crutch and a way to escape the loneliness and emptiness that consumed me. I had found myself adrift in a new country, ill-equipped for the challenges of adulthood.

Another spontaneous trip to Bali with three girlfriends would change everything. In a moment of recklessness, we decided to indulge in magic mushrooms, seeking a fleeting escape from our troubles. Little did I know, it would be a trip into the depths of my darkest fears. Sitting in a restaurant, we ordered omelettes laced with magic mushrooms. What began as a misguided attempt at adventure quickly descended into a nightmare. As the hallucinations took hold, I found myself trapped in a terrifying world of my own making. The music blared. The song was Devil Inside by INXS and I felt like I was losing my grip on reality. My friends, unaware of my torment, continued to enjoy themselves while I spiralled into chaos. Thirteen hours of hellish torment passed before the mushrooms finally wore off. My friends found me, swinging from the curtains, lost in a haze of confusion and fear.

It was a wake-up call. It was my first stark reminder of the dangers of self-destructive behaviour. I vowed to never touch drugs again. From that moment on, I embraced sobriety, determined to confront my pain head-on, rather than seeking refuge in substances.

As fate would have it, our newfound home was not to last. The house was condemned, forcing Donna and me to part ways with our friends and strike out on our own once more. Undeterred, we found a new house and advertised for a flatmate to help ease the financial burden. Interviewing potential flatmates brought unexpected surprises, none more so than the bloke I chose to move in. It was a decision that would alter the course of my life in ways I could never have imagined. He would become my husband.

Healing in Practice

Leaving home is a massive step for any young adult. It marks the shift from relying on others to standing on your own two feet—a mix of excitement and nerves. But for those of us who never felt that strong bond growing up, it can be a real struggle.

Understanding attachment is key here. It's that deep emotional connection you usually form with a parent or caregiver. It's what makes you feel safe and secure, giving you the confidence to take on the world. But if you didn't get that as a kid, leaving home can feel like stepping off a cliff into the unknown. When you've grown up without that secure attachment, you might find yourself facing some tough challenges. The idea of being independent sounds great, but the reality can hit hard. Without a solid support system, the world seems unpredictable and scary.

For example, making new friends or starting relationships can be tricky. Trusting people doesn't come easily, which can leave you feeling isolated and lonely. Without a model for healthy relationships, it's easy to feel lost and unsure of how to connect with others.

Then there's the issue of self-esteem. Secure attachment helps build a positive self-image, but if you didn't have that, you might struggle with feeling good about yourself. Doubts creep in, making you question your abilities and whether you deserve success and happiness. Facing this transition without that foundation of secure attachment is tough. Anxiety becomes a constant companion, making what should be an exciting time feel daunting and overwhelming. It's not just about moving out; it's about trying to find your place in the world without that sense of safety and belonging.

For me, leaving New Zealand at 19 was meant to be a fresh start, a chance to find myself. But the guilt and sorrow of leaving my family behind, especially Lily, weighed heavily on me. Even with all the new experiences, that sense of emptiness and longing for connection never really went away.

Finding your path and leaving home without the foundation of secure attachment is undeniably challenging, but it also presents an opportunity for growth and self-discovery. By developing awareness, developing self-compassion, practicing self-care and mastering mindfulness young adults can navigate this transition and build a fulfilling, independent life. Understand that your experiences have shaped you, and it's okay to take small steps toward growth and independence.

Remember, it's about baby steps, baby steps, baby steps. Navigating 'Inner Wealth' is having awareness in any given moment, accepting the cards you have been dealt, and setting authentic goals in the direction you value to know that it's never too late to create the connections and attachments that will support your future.

Self-Assessment Questions

Have you ever turned to unhealthy habits to cope with overwhelming emotions during a challenging period in your life? How did you eventually find your way back to a healthier path, and what did you learn about yourself in the process?

Have you ever experienced a moment of deep emotional pain during a significant separation from a loved one? How did you cope with the unspoken emotions and the silence that surrounded your family during that time?

Have you ever had a wake-up call that led you to make a significant change in your life? How did this experience shape your path toward healing and personal growth?

Chapter 6

Losing Owen

It was a typical Wednesday evening in Perth, Australia, back in 1988. I remember it clearly because the clock had just struck 5:30, and I was in the kitchen, preparing dinner. The aroma of cauliflower cheese and steak filled the room, a hearty meal to end the day. The phone rang, its sharp tone slicing through the calm of the evening. My dad was on the other end of the line, and somehow, I knew it was bad news.

"What's wrong?" I asked, my heart pounding. His words were heavy with sorrow.

"Owen is gone." His voice was strained, barely holding back the emotion.

The shock of those words left me reeling, my mind struggling to comprehend the enormity of what he had just said. My partner ran into the kitchen, drawn by the urgency of my guttural cries. In that moment, as I tried to make sense of the incomprehensible, he became my anchor, guiding me through the tsunami of emotions that threatened to engulf me.

The details were sparse, delivered in my father's usual blunt tone but muddied in a blur of disbelief and despair. Owen had taken his own life. He had hung himself in the family garage. It

Chapter 6   Losing Owen

was a fact that seemed impossible to reconcile with the gentle little boy I had known him to be. Owen and I had shared a bond forged in the crucible of siblinghood that I had thought transcended the boundaries of time and distance. The news of his passing left me speechless, grappling with a grief so deep that words seemed inadequate to express it. I couldn't speak. As I hung up the phone, the world around me blurred into a haze of shock and disbelief. My mind, numbed by the weight of grief, struggled to process the news.

In the days that followed, the weight of grief bore down on me with an intensity that threatened to suffocate me, and I couldn't sleep. It was my new partner at the time who took charge, organising the logistics of my trip back home for Owen's funeral. With every detail meticulously planned, I boarded a plane on a Thursday night, bound for Auckland. The flight seemed both interminable and too brief. Every moment spent in the air was a step closer to confronting a reality I wasn't prepared for. Memories of Owen played on a loop in my mind—his quiet presence, the bond we shared, the moments of unspoken understanding. Each thought felt like a fresh wound, and yet, there was a strange solace in remembering him.

I found relief in the kindness of strangers and staff who sensed the weight of sorrow that burdened me. Their presence, a silent comfort, provided a brief respite from the tumult of emotions that threatened to overwhelm me as I thought about the circumstances in which I would see my family again for the first time since I had left the previous year.

Arriving in Auckland at the stroke of midnight, I found myself in the quiet solitude of the airport. With hours to spare before my connecting flight to Napier, I settled into a chair, grappling with the enormity of the journey that lay ahead. As the first light of morning broke through the darkness, I boarded the plane to Napier. Touching down in Hawke's Bay, I hailed a cab and made my way to the family home. It was foreign and uncomfortable. It did not feel like I was coming home.

I'll never forget the mix of emotions that flooded my heart as I stood at the doorstep, preparing to face the family I had left behind. There was a sense of trepidation mingled with longing to be there for my siblings, even as I struggled to come to terms with the reality of Owen's absence. Returning home to the embrace of family should evoke feelings of warmth and comfort, but for me, it was tainted by a heavy burden of guilt. As I stepped back into the familiarity of our family routine, I couldn't shake the nagging sense of responsibility that weighed heavily on my conscience.

The moment I crossed the threshold, I was confronted with the stark reality of my siblings' plight. I saw it in their weary eyes, heard it in the hollow echoes of their greeting. They were the casualties of an upturned home, left to emotionally fend for themselves and my departure. I had made a choice to prioritize my own well-being over the needs of others. Faced with the turmoil and dysfunction of our family dynamic, I had chosen to save myself, to break free from the cycle of neglect and the despair that had plagued us for far too long. But in doing so, I had left my siblings behind.

Could I have done more? Should I have stayed and spoken up for my siblings' well-being? These questions haunted me, tormenting me with their relentless insistence. My mother hadn't greeted me at the door, and I was told she was unwell. I found her lying in bed. It was a sight so unfamiliar it sent a shiver down my spine. This was a woman who never stayed in bed, whose indomitable spirit had weathered countless storms. And yet, on this day, she lay before me, fragile and vulnerable, her facade of strength crumbling under the weight of grief. Beneath the surface, there lingered a sense of what I assumed was shame that weighed heavy on her heart.

Approaching her bedside, I reached out tentatively, unsure of how to navigate this unfamiliar terrain. And then, as if sensing my hesitation, she pulled me in for a hug. It was a gesture so unexpected that it left me reeling. In that moment, as my mother's tears mingled with my own, I felt a surge of emotions. It was an overwhelming mix of discomfort and tenderness, longing and resentment. For years, our relationship had been defined by the absence of affection, devoid of the warmth that should have bound us together. Yet here she was, holding me close, offering comfort, or asking for it. It was a gesture both foreign and unsettling. For me, it wasn't comforting. It was a stark reminder of the distance that had always existed between us.

Dressed in borrowed outfit of a green jumper and a black skirt lent to me by my new flatmate, I attended my first funeral after only a few hours of landing in the Hawkes Bay and reconnecting with my family. We sat in solemn silence as the weight of his death settled over us like a dark cloud. And yet, even in that moment of shared grief, there was no discussion and no attempt to understand the circumstances that had led to his untimely demise. The silence was suffocating. It already felt as if his memory had been erased from existence. There were little words of remembrance, few stories shared, just an eerie silence that hung over us like a shroud.

In the days that followed, Owen's death remained a taboo subject. My relationship with my family didn't improve. Conversations would halt abruptly at the mention of his name, eyes would avert, and a palpable discomfort would fill the air. It felt as though his suicide had turned the invisible barrier between us and the rest of the world into a solid barrier. We drifted apart as each of us grappled with our own pain and guilt.

I knew my parents had shifted, and they were living in a new house. Owen was staying back at the old house to make it look lived in until it sold. I found out it was the neighbours who discovered him. His concerned work colleagues walked in on them trying to resuscitate him. I did visit where he worked and I spoke to a few of Owen's work colleagues. They were very quiet and uncomfortable and scattered like mice when I arrived.

But the question remained—why did Owen do it? As I delved

deeper into my pain, I began to wonder if the primal wound had driven him to such desperate measures. For those who lack a strong attachment, who are deprived of unconditional love, the pain cuts deeper and the wounds fester, leaving behind scars that never truly heal. I often wondered if things would have been different if I had stayed. If I had been there, could I have made a difference? The guilt weighed heavy on my shoulders, a burden I carried for years.

In those days, communication was limited. There were no texts, no FaceTime calls. It was just occasional collect phone calls to my parents. I was off in Australia, living my own life, disconnected from the struggles back home. Looking back, I can't help but wonder if I could have done more. But as I embarked on my personal journey, I began to realise that people make their own choices, and sometimes those choices lead to tragedy. No number of what-ifs or regrets can change that.

The torture I endured in the aftermath of my brother's death was indescribable. I was lost in a sea of depression, anxiety and panic attacks which were all consuming, all overwhelming. It felt like I was suffocating under the weight of my grief. Unable to process the enormity of what had happened, I did what I thought was best. I boxed it away and buried it deep within the recesses of my mind. But the pain festered, gnawing away at my soul, leaving behind scars that would take years to heal.

What if I had contacted Owen more often? What if I hadn't moved to Australia? Why had Owen not reached out for help?

What if someone in the family had noticed the signs? What if Owen hadn't worked where he was or he wasn't staying in the house on his own? What if Owen had better access to support and resources? What if he had felt more loved and accepted? Why did he do this, how could he do this? The whys and what ifs are a fucking torment post suicide.

Healing in Practice

My father had quit his job as a radiographer and opened a gift shop. As part of my healing process, I wrote a letter to my father but I never gave it to him. I blamed him for Owen's death, for the cruelty and impatience he had shown towards my brother. It was a revelation, a cathartic release of pent-up emotions that had been festering for years. It didn't change anything, but it released a knot within me that began to unravel a childhood of trauma.

In our society, suicide is often seen as a taboo topic, something to be whispered about behind closed doors rather than openly discussed. This stigma can make it incredibly difficult for those of us left behind to express our grief and seek the support we desperately need. I found myself hesitant to talk about my brother, fearing judgment or misunderstanding. This silence only deepened my isolation, making the path through grief even more lonely.

To make sense of my brother's death, I immersed myself in understanding self-esteem, self-worth, adoption, suicide and mental health. I read books, attended support groups, and sought out others who had experienced similar losses. I learned that suicide is rarely the result of a single cause but is often the culmination of various factors, including mental illness, trauma, and overwhelming stress. This knowledge provided some comfort, helping me to see that my brother's decision was not a reflection of his love for us but rather a desperate attempt to escape his pain.

One of the most challenging aspects has been finding a way to honour my brother's memory while also navigating my own healing process. I realized that keeping silent about his death was not the answer. Instead, I began to speak openly about him and his struggles, sharing my story with others. This openness has been both cathartic and empowering, allowing me to break free from the isolation and stigma that surrounded his suicide.

I also learned the importance of self-compassion. The way through grief and healing is not linear, and it's crucial to be gentle with oneself during this time. Allowing myself to feel the full spectrum of emotions, without judgment, has been a vital part of my healing process. Engaging in self-care practices, such as journaling, meditation, and spending time in nature, helped me reconnect with myself and find moments of peace amidst the pain.

Twenty years later, a sense of indignation still boiled within me. The memory of the unmarked grave in the church grounds where my brother lay was an affront to everything I believed in. He deserved more than a nameless plot of earth.

He deserved to be remembered. I reached out to a friend of his, seeking support in mutual memories and shared grief. But even in our conversations, I found no peace or closure. Owen's absence loomed large, a void that could never be filled. I travelled back to New Zealand for a different reason. It was for closure, for peace, for the chance to finally lay my brother to rest with the dignity he deserved. The church's refusal to acknowledge his name was a bitter pill to swallow. I took matters into my own hands, determined to right this wrong.

I contacted the minister, pleaded my case, but to no avail. The church remained unmoved, unwilling to budge from their stance. But I refused to give up. I couldn't let Owen's memory fade into obscurity with no headstone and with no name. The thought of digging up his ashes was a desperate one, born out of a desperation for closure, for resolution. In the end, I opted for a different approach. I commissioned a plaque as a small token of remembrance for a life lost too soon. As we nailed the plaque to the bollard, a sense of peace washed over me. It was a feeling of closure and resolution. It wasn't the grand gesture I had envisioned, but it was enough. It was a step towards healing, towards finding peace amid tragedy. In the latter years in discussion with my parents the church offers a remembrance lawn which my parents chose for Owen from a place of love and a home in the sunshine and nature.

As I stood in the shadow of the tree, I knew that Owen's memory would live on, not in the silence of an unmarked grave, but in the hearts of those who loved him, forever remembered, forever cherished. My brother's death has forever changed me, but it has also deepened my understanding of the fragility of life and the importance of mental and emotional health. My experience with suicide has fuelled my passion to become a counsellor, speaker, author and transformational coach. Driven by the desire to inspire individuals to find passion and purpose no matter what card you are dealt. By sharing my story, I hope to contribute to breaking the silence surrounding suicide and to offer support to those who are navigating their own way through this complex and painful terrain.

In the end, the silence of suicide can be broken by the voices of those left behind. By speaking out, we honour the memories of our loved ones and create a space for healing and understanding. It is my hope that through sharing our stories, we can bring light to this shadowed topic and offer a safe space to others who are walking this difficult path.

Self-Assessment Questions

What specific steps can you take to begin your journey towards finding peace with a death and honouring their memory?

How do you find the courage to start speaking about your loved one's death and your struggles?

In what ways would sharing your story help you to break free from the isolation and loss associated with your grief?

Chapter 7

Security before Self

In the aftermath of Owen's passing, the man I was dating became more than just a casual partner. He became my rock. His unwavering support and presence provided me with a sense of stability amid chaos. As I grappled with the pain of loss, he stood by my side, offering comfort and understanding. With him, I found a sense of security that had eluded me for so long. He became my refuge and my safe harbor in the storm. In his arms, I found strength, and over time, I grew increasingly dependent on him.

As the grief weighed heavy on my shoulders, I made a conscious choice to prioritize safety over adventure. Gone was the spirit of exploration that once drove me forward. In its place, I sought stability and predictability. I clung to him fiercely, seeking refuge from the turmoil within. When trauma colours our past, the primary instinct becomes self-preservation. This can manifest in various ways, but one common response is the pursuit of stability through relationships. For me, this meant latching onto my partner not because of a deep, passionate love, but because he represented a safe harbor in the storm of my emotions. The unpredictability of life can be particularly unsettling for someone with a history of trauma. The very essence of trauma lies in its capacity to disrupt our sense of safety and security. Thus, in the aftermath of significant emotional upheaval, such as grief, the need for stability becomes paramount.

My partner represented everything I craved during this tumultuous period: predictability, steadiness, and a respite from the emotional chaos. He was a constant, a solid ground on which I could rebuild my sense of self. In choosing him, I wasn't necessarily choosing a romantic partner; I was choosing survival. However, this anchoring also came with a cost. By clinging to him for security, I was bypassing the deeper emotional work required for true healing. Instead of addressing the root causes of my fears and insecurities, I was using the relationship as a temporary shield against them.

In seeking security, I made significant compromises. The relationship was more about mitigating fear than fostering love. This dynamic is not uncommon among those with trauma histories. The allure of a safe, predictable relationship can overshadow the pursuit of a truly fulfilling emotional and sexual connection. While it provided the stability I needed, the relationship lacked the depth of a true love match. I did not have the maturity or understanding of this. I had previously only dated one male with little intimacy and no sex. My fear of rejection and low self-esteem had held me back from ever allowing myself from exploring these parts of myself.

Fear is a powerful motivator, and for many with a trauma

history, it can dictate many life choices. The fear of being alone, of facing the world without a safety net, can lead to clinging to relationships that offer security, even if they aren't deeply fulfilling. For me, the fear of reliving past abandonment and rejection was paralysing. The idea of navigating life without a steady partner seemed insurmountable. In this context, my partners steady presence was a refuge, a way to avoid confronting the depths of my loneliness and grief.

Together, we embarked on a new chapter of our lives, purchasing a farm in New South Wales outside Dubbo. For my partner, it was a dream come true It was a chance to live off the land and embrace the simplicity of rural life. I had a distorted picture that it would be like the show "County Practice", filled with community and connection. For me, it was a time of loneliness. Having left behind the connection and community in Darwin and the bank colleagues at Westpac Bank I had created friendships with, I felt so alone. With the vast expanse of the farm, I felt isolated and adrift. The solitude weighed heavily on my spirit, and despite my best efforts to find contentment in our new life, I struggled to find a sense of belonging. My family rarely visited, his parents and his daughter came, but seldom anyone else. The wide-open spaces that promised him freedom instead became a prison, where the echoes of abandonment and rejection reverberated around my brain.

Isolation for someone like me isn't just physical; it's emotional and psychological. As an adopted child, I had spent

Chapter 7 Security before Self

my entire life grappling with the idea of being unwanted, of being left behind. This fundamental wound, often referred to as the primal wound, colours every aspect of one's life. It creates an insatiable need for affirmation and connection, a constant search for validation to fill the void left by that initial separation. Living on the farm, I found myself cut off from the social interactions that had always been my lifeline. The friends, colleagues, and casual acquaintances that had once formed a safety net of sorts were now miles away. The farm's remoteness, while idyllic to some, was a stark reminder of my disconnection. Despite my attempts to adapt, I knew deep down that I couldn't stay.

Human beings are inherently social creatures, and for those of us with a history of trauma, this need for connection is even more pronounced. We seek out interactions, not just for companionship, but to assure ourselves that we are wanted, needed, and valued. On the farm, the isolation was more than just a lack of people; it was a stark confrontation with my deepest fears and insecurities. Without the constant reinforcement of my worth through social interactions, the old doubts and anxieties began to resurface. I felt myself slipping into a dark place, where the voices of the past whispered that I was not enough, that I was alone and always would be.

In this moment of isolation and insomnia, I realized that I couldn't sacrifice my own well-being for the sake of others. I had spent a lifetime avoiding rejection at all costs, often to the detriment of my own needs and desires. But now, faced with the stark reality of my isolation, I understood that I needed to prioritize my own mental and emotional health. Leaving the farm was not just a physical act; it was a declaration of self-worth, one of the first conscious choices. It was an acknowledgment that my need for connection and social interaction was valid and important. It was a step towards a fuller life, towards breaking the cycle of abandonment and rejection that had haunted me for so long.

We set our sights on a new chapter in Brisbane. At the age of 26, I found myself starting afresh in a bustling city, seeking structure and security in the familiarity of urban life. Returning to a more socially connected environment was essential for my well-being. It allowed me to rebuild my support network, to engage in meaningful interactions that reinforced my sense of belonging. In time I sought out random uncommitted therapy and a support group where I could share my experiences and connect with others who understood the complexities of adoption trauma.

My partner's history of failed marriages and children to ex-partners added a layer of complexity to our relationship. I knew that if we were to have a future together, children would need to be part of the equation. It was a conversation that loomed over us, lingering in the background as we navigated the ups and downs of our relationship. The topic of children had become a constant presence in our discussion. For me, it was a rollercoaster of uncertainty.

The move to Brisbane played a pivotal role in solidifying

my commitment to starting a family. It was here that I found connection in my partner's family, immersing myself in their warmth and affection. For someone who had grown up without the comfort of physical touch, their hugs and gestures of love were a revelation. It was a foreign yet deeply comforting experience. His family became my family as I enjoyed their company and began to build relationships and let love in.

But at 26, everything changed. It was as if a switch had been flipped, and suddenly, the idea of becoming a mother became a non-negotiable certainty. In my mind, there was a strong belief in the traditional notion that marriage should precede parenthood. Reflecting on my decision to marry at such a young age, I couldn't help but wonder if I had rushed into it too quickly. In hindsight, perhaps I had. But at the time, I was consumed by a sense of urgency.

If it hadn't been for my sister, I don't know how I would have made it through some of my fears. With only $5 to her name, she had landed on our doorstep from New Zealand just before my wedding, to be bridesmaid, seeking respite from the storm that had long been brewing in our family. I had helped her get on her feet and she was thriving being on her own. She offered her unwavering support and companionship and in return, I loved her as hard as I could.

For me, marrying was more than just a declaration of love. It was a lifeline, a chance to find stability and security in a world that often felt chaotic and unpredictable. The wedding day arrived with the sharing of the vows at an Anglican Church in Alexander Hills and the celebration at Whepstead Manor in Wellington Point, Brisbane. Mum, Dad, oldest brother, his family and Jenny made it special. Underneath the wedding dress, flowers, food and cake was fear and anxiety with the spotlight on me. Not use to a fuss or abundance of food and fun it was a foreboding feeling. Was I doing the right decision, making the right choice? Will everyone have a great time? I felt so young and unequipped for this momentous decision. However, with him by my side, I felt a sense of peace and contentment that I had never known before. My focus shifted towards a new purpose: motherhood. It was a longing that I knew I would experience one day and the decisions I was making was bringing it closer.

Healing in Practice

Journaling can be a powerful tool for people who struggle to be their authentic selves. Here's how it helps:

1. **Self-Reflection:**
   - Understanding Feelings: Writing down thoughts and feelings helps in identifying and understanding emotions that might be suppressed or ignored.
   - Recognising Patterns: Journaling allows for the recognition of patterns in thoughts and behaviours, highlighting areas where one might be pretending or not being true to themselves.

2. Clarity and Insight:

- Sorting Thoughts: It helps in sorting through the clutter of daily thoughts, providing clarity on what truly matters to the individual.
- Insight into Desires: By regularly writing, individuals can gain insight into their true desires, values, and aspirations, which might be hidden under societal expectations or peer pressure.

3. Emotional Release:

- Safe Space: Journaling provides a safe space to express feelings without fear of judgment or criticism, allowing for genuine self-expression.
- Cathartic Experience: Writing can be a cathartic experience, helping to release pent-up emotions and stress.

4. Building Confidence:

- Validating Experiences: When individuals see their thoughts and feelings on paper, it can validate their experiences and make them feel heard, even if only by themselves.
- Empowerment: Regular journaling can empower individuals by helping them to see their growth and progress over time, boosting self-esteem and confidence in their true selves.

5. Problem-Solving:

- Exploring Solutions: Writing about problems and challenges can help in exploring solutions and different perspectives, aiding in more authentic decision-making.
- Reflecting on Choices: It allows for reflection on past choices and their alignment with one's true self, guiding future actions.

6. Goal Setting and Accountability:

- Setting Authentic Goals: Journaling helps in setting goals that align with one's true desires and values rather than external expectations.
- Tracking Progress: It provides a way to track progress and hold oneself accountable, ensuring that actions remain true to personal goals and values.

Practical Examples:

- Daily Reflections: Spending a few minutes each day writing about feelings and experiences can reveal true emotions and desires.
- Gratitude Journaling: Listing things you are grateful for can highlight what truly matters to you.
- Prompted Journaling: Using prompts like "What would I do if I weren't afraid?" or "What are my core values?" can uncover authentic thoughts and aspirations.

- Writing Letters: Writing letters to your future or past self can help in understanding and accepting your true self.

Journaling fosters a deeper connection by providing a space for honest reflection and emotional expression. It helps individuals understand and embrace their true selves, leading to a more authentic and fulfilling life.

Self-Assessment Questions

Have you ever made an important life decision out of a sense of urgency or longing? Looking back, how do you feel about that decision, and what did you learn from the experience?

Have you ever found that a place or situation you thought would bring freedom instead of intensified feelings of abandonment or rejection? How did you navigate and heal from those lingering wounds?

Have you ever made a significant move to a new place seeking a fresh start? How did the transition from one environment to another impact your sense of self and belonging?

Chapter 8

A Family of My Own

For many adoptees, but also many women, the experience of having a child can stir up unresolved feelings of loss, abandonment, and identity. The desire to provide a stable and loving environment for our children often intersects with the need to confront our own pasts and to make sense of our own experiences of being adopted and to reconcile them with the responsibilities of parenthood. If I was going to become a mother, I wanted to find my own.

My first son's arrival into the world was marked by a journey that began long before his first breath, intertwined with my own struggles and fears. As I carried him within me, every moment of my pregnancy was filled with a sense of wonder and love. I embraced the changes in my body, glowing with the anticipation of welcoming new life into the world. But as the time for his birth drew near, the joy I had felt was overshadowed by the looming sense of fear.

From the moment I discovered I was pregnant, I was consumed by a sense of dread that history would repeat itself, that the love I held in my arms would one day slip through my fingers. It was a fear that gnawed at the edges of my consciousness, whispering tales of loss and abandonment in the dead of night. I hardly slept.

The day of his birth began with the rupture of my waters at home. As the hours passed, the intensity of the contractions increased, and with it, so did my anxiety. I watched in disbelief as my husband tended to mundane tasks outside as I grappled with closer contractions. In that moment, his actions felt like a reminder of the isolation I felt in my own pain. My mind was plagued by a sense of unpreparedness, not just physically but emotionally.

By the time we reached the hospital, a menacing fear gripped me as I faced the unknown. And when the moment finally came for my child to enter the world, the experience turned from fear to sheer terror. The use of forceps, coupled with the absence of pain relief, plunged me into a state of shock and trauma. I felt violated, as if my body had been subjected to a brutality that left me emotionally numb and disconnected. In the aftermath of my son's birth, I found myself grappling with a numbness that lingered long after the physical pain had subsided. For weeks, I remained in a state of shock, unable to process the events that had unfolded.

Despite being pregnant herself Jenny, selflessly put aside her own needs to care for me. It was a true testament to the depth of our sibling bond. Within three months of having my son, she then had her son. I was so terrified for her because I thought everybody had the same experience as me. But fortunately, her birth was fine.

As I cradled my first-born son in my arms, and the shock subsiding, his tiny fingers wrapped around mine, I felt a wave of overwhelming love wash over me. He was the embodiment of innocence, a precious gift that I had longed for with all my heart. Yet, beneath the surface of this love lurked a shadow that threatened to consume me whole.

He was the easiest baby, his gentle coos and infectious giggles filling our home with joy. And yet, as I gazed into his innocent eyes, I couldn't shake the gnawing fear that gripped my heart. It was a fear born from the depths of my own past, a fear of rejection that had haunted me since the day I first understood what it means to be adopted. As he grew, so too did my fears. With each passing day, I found myself grappling with the relentless fear of rejection, haunted by the ghosts of my own past. I had bonded with him in the womb, felt his every movement as if it were my own, and yet, the fear of losing him loomed large in my mind and heart. As I gazed into his crib, I felt a wave of apprehension wash over me, the fear that if I gave him my heart, the unthinkable would happen.

For adoptees like me, the fear of rejection is a constant companion, a shadow that follows us wherever we go. It is a fear born from the depths of our own trauma, a fear that threatens to unravel the fragile tapestry of our newfound happiness. And yet, despite the overwhelming weight of this fear, I knew that I had to confront it head-on. Slowly, tentatively, I began to let my son in, allowing myself to fully embrace the depth of love that filled my heart. Looking back now, I can see

Chapter 8   A Family of My Own

how his birth became a catalyst for confronting the trauma of my past. As I held my son in my arms, I knew that his arrival had forever changed me, marking the beginning of a time of healing and growth.

My first son was born with a wisdom that belied his years. He was an old soul wrapped in the innocence of infancy. In his presence, I found a strength that I never knew existed, drawing energy and resilience from the tiny bundle cradled in my arms. Despite my fears, his presence became a source of calmness in the darkness of my inner turmoil.

The arrival of my parents, eager to share in the joy of my son's birth, only served to exacerbate my anxiety. Their presence, though well-intentioned, stirred up a whirlwind of emotions of longing, resentment, anxiety and unspoken pain. As they filled our home with their familiar presence, I felt the weight of unresolved trauma pressing down on me, suffocating the joy that should have filled the air.

In those early days, as I struggled to emerge from the fog of shock and trauma of the birth, I found calm in the simple moments like the quiet hum of the television or the gentle rhythm of my son's breath as he slept. Alone in my thoughts, I grappled with the challenges of motherhood, navigating the complexities of raising a child while confronting the demons of my past. Despite the challenges that lay ahead, my son remained a constant source of strength and inspiration. He was a reminder that even in the darkest moments, love has the power to heal and transform. As I embarked on this minefield of motherhood, I knew that with him in my world I would find the courage to confront my past and embrace the future with open arms.

The 10-year veto had expired, and on that very day I made the decision to apply for my original birth certificate. With trembling hands, I entered the post office, anticipation bubbling within me like a dormant volcano ready to erupt. The clerk handed me the document, and as I traced my fingers over the letters spelling out "Maria Smith," I felt a surge of emotion welling up inside me. Maria Smith was a name that had once belonged to me, the only thing ever given to me by my mother. But as I scanned the lines of text, my heart sank. There, beneath my name, was a glaring omission—the absence of my father's details. It was a void that gnawed at the edges of my consciousness, a silent reminder of the unanswered questions that lingered in the depths of my soul.

Determined to uncover the truth, I would concentrate on my mother first. I reached out to the adoption agency in New Zealand. With their help, I tracked down my biological mother's address. A lifeline dangled precariously before me, offering the promise of closure and reconciliation. After many failed attempts, I penned a letter to my long-lost mother, pouring my heart and soul onto the page, sharing the intricacies of my life with a stranger who held the key to my identity. I spoke of my precious son, a beacon of light in the shadowy corridors of my past.

Days turned into a week, and at last, a response arrived 15

Chapter 8   A Family of My Own

days later. It was a handwritten letter bearing the weight of a lifetime of regret and longing. With bated breath, I tore open the envelope, eager to bridge the chasm that separated us. But as I read her words, my heart shattered into a million pieces. My biological mother, a young woman on a working holiday from England in New Zealand, had an affair with a married man. Three months after the brief liaison, she discovered she was pregnant. Faced with the daunting prospect of single motherhood, she chose to stay in New Zealand, to carry me to term and give birth to me. Even though she made the brave decision to bring me into the world, she knew that she was not equipped to raise a child on her own and decided to put me up for adoption.

Within four years of my birth, my biological mother married a man who would become the father of my two half-sisters. After four short years of their marriage, he passed away unexpectedly, leaving my mother to raise their children on her own. And so, once again, she found herself thrust into the role of a single parent—a role she had thought she had left behind forever.

"You are in my past," she wrote, "and that is where I want to keep you." It was a rejection so painful, so final, that I struggled to comprehend its magnitude.

As I read the letter, a wave of disbelief and sorrow washed over me. The closure I had sought for so long seemed suddenly elusive, slipping through my fingers like grains of sand. The hope that had buoyed me through years of searching now faltered, replaced by emptiness. Her rejection pierced deep into the core of my being, reopening old wounds and reigniting dormant insecurities. I had spent a lifetime yearning for her to come and claim me, hoping against hope that she would welcome me into her world with open arms. Yet here I was, faced with the stark reality that she had chosen to give me away.

For months, I wrestled with anger, sadness, and an overwhelming sense of abandonment. Questions swirled in my mind. Did I not deserve her love? Was I unworthy of her acceptance? The pain of her rejection cut deeper than any wound I had ever known. Yet, I couldn't accept that she didn't want a relationship with me and continued to keep writing to her. I knew that closure was not something I could find in her acceptance or rejection. It lay within my own ability to reconcile the past with the present, to forge a path forward despite the heartache that threatened to consume me

With the birth of my second son 18 months later, there was a new set of challenges. He was a breech birth, but it was a beautiful birthing experience. Determined for it to be different second time around I was numbed with an epidural in a private hospital. This was done in the first stage of labour, so I had a painless delivery. As he grew into a toddler with colic, reflux, middle ear infections, delayed speech and struggles with learning and auditory processing, his needs become particularly demanding, requiring a level of care and attention that left me feeling drained and overwhelmed. And

Chapter 8   A Family of My Own

with my husband often absent, the workload fell squarely on my shoulders.

Before the arrival of our children, the dynamic of our marriage was one of me constantly striving to please him and him providing financially for me. But as the demands of parenthood set in, a subtle undercurrent of resentment began to simmer beneath the surface. The demands of parenthood exacerbated the cracks in our relationship, laying bare the stark reality of our roles. Unable to voice my frustrations, I internalized my feelings, burying them deep within me. As the ultimate pleaser, I was accustomed to putting others' needs before my own, even at the expense of my own emotional well-being. And so, the resentment began to fester, a silent poison that seeped into every aspect of our relationship. The lack of communication only served to exacerbate the growing divide between us. I longed to express my feelings, to seek understanding and validation from him, but the words remained trapped inside me, stifled by fear and the ingrained belief that my needs were secondary to his and fear of rejection was too great.

With each passing year, the resentment grew, fuelled by unmet expectations and unspoken grievances. I watched as he poured himself into his work, providing for his family, seemingly oblivious to the strain his absence placed on our family. And with each missed milestone, each late night on a job or in the shed, the distance between us widened. And as the years passed, it became increasingly difficult to ignore the growing chasm between us. I had never learned how to express my feelings, how to give voice to the chaos raging inside me. Growing up in a household where emotions were stifled and buried beneath layers of silence, I had internalized the belief that my thoughts and feelings were unworthy of acknowledgment, destined to remain hidden in the shadows of my subconscious.

Attempts to breach the walls of silence that surrounded us were met with indifference or hostility, leaving me feeling even more isolated and alone. We danced around the edges of conflict, tiptoeing around the elephant in the room, *I* was too afraid to confront the demons lurking in the shadows. I found myself sinking deeper into despair, the weight of my unspoken burdens dragging me down into the depths of a dark and lonely abyss. Raising two little boys amid this turmoil felt like an insurmountable task, a Herculean feat for which I was ill-equipped and unprepared.

Healing in Practice

As an adoptee, navigating relationships can often feel like traversing a minefield, fraught with hidden triggers and unspoken fears. From childhood, we learn to navigate the world with a sense of detachment, our attachment systems wired to expect loss and abandonment at every turn. Psychologists have long studied the impact of adoption on attachment and relationships, shedding light on the complex interplay between early life experiences and adult relational patterns. The work of renowned psychologist John Bowlby laid the foundation for understanding attachment theory, which posits that our early experiences with caregivers shape our ability to form and maintain relationships throughout life.

The absence of biological ties can leave a gaping hole in their sense of self, leading to feelings of insecurity and fear of rejection. This insecurity often manifests in adult relationships, where adoptees may struggle to trust and connect with others on a deep emotional level. My husband's emotional unavailability and physical absence triggered deep-seated attachment wounds, leaving me with the familiar feeling of being adrift in a sea of loneliness and longing. Unable to articulate my needs and fears, I found myself trapped in a cycle of emotional disconnection, where conflict was avoided at all costs for fear of further rejection.

Research has shown that adoptees are more likely to experience difficulties in forming secure attachments and maintaining healthy relationships. A study conducted by psychologist David Brodzinsky found that adoptees are at increased risk for attachment-related issues, such as fear of abandonment, difficulty expressing emotions, and challenges in establishing trust. From the outset, I had found motherhood daunting. My own upbringing had not provided the best role model for nurturing and compassion. My mother's approach to parenting was rooted in practicality, control and routine: the house was always clean, meals were cooked, laundry was done, and homework was supervised. While these are essential aspects of parenting, they lacked the warmth, connection, and emotional support that children need to truly thrive and love was conditional.

Instinctively, I replicated my mother's methods, focusing on the coordination of raising children. I maintained a clean house, ensured the boys were fed and clothed, and managed their educational needs. However, I struggled immensely with the softer side of parenting—the nurturing, the loving, the slowing down to connect on a deeper level. It wasn't that I didn't want to be a loving, compassionate mother; it was that I didn't know how.

Self-Assessment Questions

How do you cope with feelings of insecurity or fear of rejection in your relationships, and what strategies have helped you build deeper emotional connections with others?

Which relationships in your life have been the most reciprocal and nurturing? How have these connections contributed to your sense of self-worth and happiness?

Have you ever faced a decision from someone you cared about that was hard to accept? How did this experience affect your feelings of abandonment and rejection, and what steps did you take to cope with these emotions?

Chapter 9

Shifting Sands

Four years after my second son was born, my youngest son arrived. I always knew I wanted another child, and he completed our family. He was a contented baby, affectionate and loving who fitted into our busy household. Despite the struggles, there were beautiful, special times that punctuated the noise and busyness. My boys taught me how to love in ways I had never experienced. They craved cuddles and physical affection, something that felt foreign to me but which I slowly learned to give.

Bit by bit, my sons broke through the tough exterior I'd built around myself. Their innocent need for love and connection made me face my own emotional walls. They showed me how to cuddle, how to be affectionate, and how to show love in a way that actually meant something. These moments were priceless, slowly changing me into a more emotionally present and connected mum.

Looking back, motherhood was just as much about my own growth as it was about raising my boys. Each of them, in their own way, helped me give love and grow. They pushed me to break free from old patterns and to carve out a new path, one that embraced vulnerability and connection. Through them, I learned that love isn't just about meeting physical needs but also about being emotionally available and truly present.

I remember those early days vividly. My eldest, with his boundless contented energy, always wanted hugs and snuggles. At first, it felt awkward, but his persistence paid off. Then came the bedtime stories with my middle child, where his need for comfort made me realise the importance of emotional closeness. My youngest, with his innocent questions and endless curiosity, made me see the world through a softer, more open lens.

The school runs, the playdates, and the quiet moments at home all added layers to my understanding of what it meant to be a mum. It wasn't just about feeding them, dressing them, and keeping them safe. It was about being there for them, really being there, in the moments that mattered. Their laughter, their tears, and their simple joys taught me that emotional presence is the heart of parenting.

In the end, my sons didn't just make me a mother; they made me a better person. They taught me that it's okay to be vulnerable, to show emotion, and to connect deeply. They showed me that love is about more than just being there; it's about truly being present, every single day. Raising three sons was undeniably hard, but it was also incredibly rewarding. They were my teachers in the truest sense, guiding me towards a fuller, more loving version of myself. While I navigated the complexities of motherhood, they provided the unconditional

Chapter 9 Shifting Sands

love and acceptance that I had longed for, helping me to become the mother they deserved and the person I needed to be.

I was still sending letters and photographs to my biological mother, sharing glimpses of my life and family in the hopes that something might spark a connection. Each letter was filled with hope and longing, and each photograph was a testament to the life I was building despite the deep void I felt. But instead of the response I yearned for, I was met with returned letters. The pain of these rejections was heartbreaking, yet I continued to subject myself to this emotional turmoil. It took me several years to recognize the trauma I was inflicting upon myself by repeatedly reaching out to someone who had made it clear she did not want to be a part of my life.

This period was marked by a relentless cycle of hope and heartbreak. Each letter I sent carried the weight of my expectations and the pain of my past. When my letters were returned unopened, it felt like a fresh wound, a stark reminder of her rejection. Despite this, I persisted, driven by the belief that she owed me a relationship simply because she was my biological mother. The realization that she did not share this belief was a bitter pill to swallow. The societal and personal expectations I held that a mother should want to know her child clashed painfully with my reality. I struggled to accept her decision, and this struggle exacerbated my sense of abandonment and rejection.

It was only in my mid-30s that I began to understand the necessity of acceptance. The process was neither quick nor easy. I had to confront the harsh reality that my biological mother had the right to her own choices, including the choice to not have a relationship with me. This acceptance was pivotal in my wellbeing, but it was fraught with emotional battles and a deep sense of loss. Stopping the letters and letting go was one of the hardest decisions I made. I wanted to give up on a part of myself, on a dream that I had held close for so long. But it was also a crucial step in moving forward. By no longer subjecting myself to the pain of her rejections, I began to reclaim my emotional well-being. I started to understand that her decision was not a reflection of my worth but of her own circumstances and choices.

This time in my life taught me a great deal about acceptance and the importance of self-compassion. I learned that I could not force a relationship where there was no willingness on the other side. This realization, painful as it was, allowed me to begin the process of acceptance and to focus on the relationships in my life that were reciprocal and nurturing.

In the years that followed, I shifted my energy towards building a strong, supportive family with my husband and children. The love and connection I cultivated with them became the foundation of my emotional recovery. While the absence of a relationship with my biological mother remained a source of sorrow, it no longer defined my sense of self or my capacity for happiness. It taught me the power of letting go and the importance of embracing the love and connections that were present in my life, rather than fixating on those

Chapter 9 Shifting Sands

that were not. My initial thinking was if I find my biological mother I will find me, I knew I had to find me on my own.

There were moments of pure joy and family bliss. The days spent camping under the stars, taking day trips, and hosting family barbecues are etched in my memory as some of the happiest times of our lives. Yet, beneath the veneer of domestic bliss, there was always a simmering undercurrent of discontent. To the outside world, we seemed like the epitome of marital harmony, a picture-perfect family living the suburban dream. But behind closed doors, a different story unfolded. Little seeds of unhappiness and resentment took root within me, slowly winding their way through the cracks in our seemingly idyllic facade.

I carried these seeds of discontent deep in my soul, unwilling and not knowing how to voice the growing unease gnawing at my spirit. The fear of confrontation, of rocking the boat, kept me silent, even as the weight of my unspoken grievances threatened to crush me. Whenever I dared to voice my feelings or express the turmoil raging within me, I was met with anger and annoyance. My attempts at communication were often greeted with stony silence, leaving me feeling isolated and alone. My husband's silence echoed my mother's silent treatment, reverberating through the walls of our home—a painful reminder of the trauma that had shaped my formative years.

I remember vividly the nights when I lay awake, staring at the ceiling, feeling the heavy cloak of dissatisfaction settle over me. During the day, I'd put on a brave face, laughing and smiling as if everything was perfect. But at night, in the quiet darkness, my true feelings would surface, and I'd grapple with the loneliness that seemed to envelop me. The discontent was like a silent companion, always present, always whispering doubts and fears into my ear.

It wasn't just the big things that caused the cracks to appear—it was the little things too. The small, everyday interactions that should have brought us closer instead drove us further apart. A missed glance, a half-hearted hug, or a distracted nod—all these tiny moments added up, building a wall of emotional distance between us. I tried to bridge that gap, the emotional gap, to reach out and connect, but my efforts often felt futile.

In those moments of despair, I'd think back to the happy times—the laughter around the campfire, the joy of discovering new places on our day trips, the warmth of family gatherings. Those memories became a lifeline, reminding me that happiness was possible, even if it felt out of reach at that moment.

The silence and emotional disconnect between us continued to grow, echoing the unspoken words and unresolved feelings. I realised that I was not just battling the discontent within my marriage, but also the ghosts of my past. The patterns of silence and avoidance that I had learned in my childhood were replaying themselves in my adult life, trapping me in a cycle of unhappiness.

Around this same time, my shopping addiction really took

hold. While some people turn to alcohol, drugs, or other substances to cope with their issues, I turned to shopping. My husband's income provided a comfortable lifestyle, and money was never a concern. This financial security, combined with my lack of personal fulfillment, led me to chase a dopamine hit in buying clothes. Shopping became my escape, a way to momentarily fill the void inside me. It was a temporary high, a distraction from the pain and emptiness I felt. I didn't have a healthy relationship with money; it was merely a tool to soothe my emotional wounds. The shopping addiction flared up as a symptom of my deeper issues, a tangible manifestation of my internal struggles.

My husband, who worked long hours to provide for the family, was largely unaware of the extent of my addiction. The emotional connection I desperately needed was lacking, and the shopping provided a false sense of comfort and control. It was a vicious cycle: the more I shopped, the more I felt guilty and ashamed, which only fuelled my need to shop more. Through therapy, I began to understand the underlying causes of my addiction. The feelings of inadequacy and the constant self-doubt were driving my need to find external validation through material possessions. Recognizing this pattern was the first step towards breaking free from it.

My relationship with money was complex and troubled. I didn't understand its value, which led to reckless spending and a deeply ingrained shopping addiction. This addiction wasn't just a fleeting phase; it was a powerful and persistent force in my life, beginning when I was just 14 and finally waning when I reached 51. For nearly four decades, shopping was my go-to coping mechanism whenever I felt low, isolated, or struggled with my self-esteem. The origins of my shopping addiction were rooted in the same feelings of isolation and loneliness that plagued me throughout my life. As a teenager, shopping provided a brief escape from the emotional turmoil I experienced. It was a way to feel a sense of control and momentarily lift my spirits. The thrill of buying new clothes, the instant gratification of acquiring something new, and the temporary boost in confidence were all potent forces that kept me returning to the stores. Shopping became a form of self-medication, offering a fleeting high that helped mask deeper issues.

As I moved into my 30s and 40s, the addiction only grew stronger. It was during these years, particularly when my boys were young, that my shopping habits became most pronounced. The pressures of motherhood, coupled with my unresolved emotional struggles, intensified my need to escape through shopping. Whenever I felt overwhelmed or unworthy, I would head to the stores and indulge in buying clothes. Each purchase was a hit of dopamine, providing a temporary rush of happiness and relief from my inner turmoil.

However, the relief was always short-lived. The thrill of a new purchase would quickly fade, leaving me craving more. This cycle of craving and temporary satisfaction kept me hooked. It wasn't just about acquiring new items; it was about the emotional release and the brief moments of feeling good about myself. But inevitably, the guilt and shame would follow, especially when I realized how selfish my behaviour had become. I often bought for myself rather than for my children, a reflection of my desperate need to fill the void within me.

Looking back, I can see how destructive this pattern was. My addiction to shopping was a symptom of deeper issues that I hadn't addressed. It was a way to avoid dealing with my low self-esteem, my feelings of isolation, and the emotional pain that had been with me since childhood. Despite the temporary relief it provided, the long-term consequences were damaging. Financially, it was irresponsible, and emotionally, it kept me from truly addressing the root causes of my unhappiness. This has taught me a lot about addiction and self-worth. Shopping was my escape, my way of coping with feelings of inadequacy and isolation. But it was also a prison, keeping me from addressing the real issues in my life.

I'd retreat to my comfy couch, the metaphor for both physically and mentally shutting down and withdrawing from the world around me. It became a place where I could hide my pain, even from myself. I would sit there, my energy drained, fatigued, trying to numb the emotional turmoil inside. The more I buried my feelings, the more they festered, creating an internal storm that seemed impossible to calm.

During those dark moments, I'd replay the past, scrutinizing every interaction, every argument, every silent treatment. I'd wonder if there was something I could have done differently, if there was a way to break the cycle. But the answers eluded me, buried under layers of self-doubt and fear. The comfy couch in a bizarre way became both a refuge and a prison, offering a temporary escape from reality while simultaneously trapping me in my own thoughts.

I remember one particularly rough week when I barely connected with anyone and had shut down. "Don't look at me, don't come near me and definitely don't touch me." My boys would come home from school, their innocent faces full of questions I couldn't answer. They'd ask me what was wrong, why I seemed so sad, and I'd force a smile, telling them everything was fine. But deep down, I knew they could see through the facade. They could sense the pain I was trying so hard to hide, and their concern only added to my guilt.

Living with this constant self-doubt was exhausting. Every action, every decision was clouded by the fear that I wasn't good enough. This mindset was deeply ingrained, and it stemmed from a lifetime of internalizing negative beliefs about myself. When you elevate someone else to a pedestal, you simultaneously diminish your own worth. This was my reality, and it was a suffocating way to live.

Another area in my life I struggled with was discipline. The thought of my children rejecting me was unbearable. The deep-seated fear of rejection, a common issue among adoptees, made it nearly impossible for me to enforce rules or boundaries. I found myself constantly vacillating, unable to stand firm. I was so submissive and lenient that my boys quickly learned they could walk all over me. The mere idea of them turning away from me, of losing their love or approval, was paralysing.

This fear-driven inability to discipline created a significant imbalance in our household. My husband was forced to take on the role of the disciplinarian. He had to be the one to set and enforce rules, which placed a heavy burden on him. Our partnership suffered because of this imbalance. We weren't functioning as a cohesive team, which is crucial when raising three active boys. Instead of presenting a united front, we were divided, and the boys could sense this division.

The strain on our relationship grew. My husband felt unsupported and overwhelmed, as he had to shoulder the responsibility of maintaining discipline. Meanwhile, I felt trapped by my fears and unable to contribute effectively to parenting in this crucial area. This division not only affected our relationship as a couple but also influenced the dynamics within our family. Our inability to function as a team made parenting more challenging and stressful.

During this period, I was still in the process of growing into adulthood myself. Despite being a mother, I was grappling with my unresolved issues and trying to find my footing. The responsibility of raising three boys while dealing with my own emotional turmoil was overwhelming. I often felt like I was floundering, trying to balance my personal growth with the demands of motherhood. My inability to discipline effectively and my fear of speaking up and rejection weren't isolated issues; they were deeply intertwined with my own sense of self-worth and unresolved trauma.

The comfy couch, a metaphor for my unhealthy thinking wasn't just a place; it was a state of mind. It was the embodiment of all the unresolved emotions and unspoken words that had accumulated over the years. It was where I went when I felt overwhelmed, where I retreated when the world became too much to bear. But it was also where I began to realize that something had to change.

A small voice inside me began to whisper that it was time to break free. It was time to confront the patterns of my past and find a way to heal. The comfy couch had served its purpose, but it was no longer enough. I needed to find a way to truly connect with my emotions, to validate my own experiences, and to start living authentically.

At 36, with my oldest child being eight, I reached a pivotal moment in my life. The years of unspoken pain and unresolved trauma culminated in a period of intense anger and emotional exhaustion. I was overwhelmed, feeling more like a worn-out shell than a person. The anger was consuming, and I felt disconnected from myself and my children. This period marked a turning point for me, one that would lead to significant change and healing.

I had become irritable and short-tempered, often lashing out in ways that were reminiscent of my own mother's harshness. The realization that I was becoming the very person I had struggled with growing up was terrifying. Worse yet, I began

Chapter 9   Shifting Sands

to see my late brother Owen in my eldest son. This blurred the lines between past and present, making my reactions more intense and confusing. It was in this frightening space that I knew I needed professional help.

Reaching out for the right therapy felt like a leap into the unknown, as I had attempted this previously, but I was desperate for change. My first session where I was fully committed was a mixture of nerves and relief, as I began to unpack the layers of pain and anger that had accumulated over the years. The therapist helped me understand that my anger was a mask for deeper emotions – grief, fear, and loss.

Week by week, I started to unravel the tangled web of my past. I revisited old wounds and faced painful memories head-on. The process was exhausting but necessary. I learned about the impact of my childhood experiences on my adult life, and how the unresolved trauma had shaped my responses and behaviour. It was like piecing together a jigsaw puzzle of my emotional landscape, one painful piece at a time.

My therapist also introduced me to mindfulness and self-compassion practices. These tools became lifelines, helping me to begin staying grounded and present, even when the weight of my emotions threatened to pull me under. I began to notice the small, everyday moments of connection and joy with my children that I had previously overlooked in my haze of anger and exhaustion.

One afternoon, during a quiet moment in the garden, my eldest son came up to me with a drawing he had made. It was a simple picture of our family, with everyone holding hands and smiling. He looked up at me, his eyes full of hope and innocence, and said, "I love you, Mum." In that moment, something shifted inside me. The anger and frustration melted away, replaced by a deep sense of love and gratitude. I realised that despite my struggles, I was still capable of giving and receiving love.

With time and therapy, I began to rebuild my relationship with my children. I apologised for the times I had been harsh and explained that I was working on becoming a better parent. To my surprise, they responded with understanding and forgiveness, teaching me that it's never too late to change and grow.

This journey of healing also involved confronting my grief over Owen's death. I allowed myself to mourn him properly, acknowledging the impact his loss had on me. I talked about him with my therapist, sharing memories and shedding tears that had been held back for too long. This process was incredibly painful but also deeply cathartic.

As I accepted, I found new ways to honour Owen's memory. I told my children stories about their uncle, keeping his spirit alive in our family. We planted a tree in the garden, a living tribute to him, symbolising growth and renewal.

Now, looking back, I see that reaching out for help was the bravest thing I could have done. It not only saved me, but it rippled thru to my family. I learned that it's okay to be vulnerable, to ask for support, and to take steps towards healing, no matter how difficult they may seem.

Healing in Practice

At 36, I embarked on getting to know myself and how I tick and has changed my life. I've learned to forgive myself and to embrace the imperfections that make us human. Most importantly, I've connected deeper with my children, creating a loving and supportive environment where we can all thrive. The road to healing is ongoing, but with each step, I move closer to a place of peace and acceptance.

The decision to seek intensive counselling was not an easy one. Admitting that I needed help felt like a failure, but I was desperate. I found a counsellor and began therapy. The first three sessions were spent in tears. For the first time, I allowed someone to see the raw, unfiltered pain that I had kept hidden for so long. It was both liberating and terrifying.

The counsellor sat opposite me, providing a safe space to express my unhappiness, anger, and loneliness. This was a revelation. I had always felt that struggle and suffering were isolating experiences, but here was someone who validated my feelings and offered support without judgment. This validation was something I had never experienced before. I had always minimised how I felt.

During these sessions, I began to unravel the deeply rooted beliefs that had governed my self-perception. I came to understand how these beliefs were contributing to my depression and anxiety, which had gone undiagnosed for years. The counsellor helped me see that I had internalized a lot of harmful messages: that I was not good enough, that I did not belong, that I was a mistake, and that I was not important. These beliefs had kept my self-esteem low and perpetuated a cycle of negativity.

The work with my counsellor marked the beginning of a new chapter. She helped me confront and challenge my core beliefs, laying the groundwork for building my self-esteem. This process was not quick or easy, but it was essential. I began to see that my worth was not determined by my past or by the mistakes I had made. This period of intense self-examination and growth was transformative. It allowed me to start healing the wounds of my past and to begin building a healthier, more compassionate relationship with myself and my children. The healing was ongoing, and there were still many challenges to face, but for the first time, I felt a glimmer of hope.

This turning point was a critical step towards liking myself. It taught me the importance of seeking help and the power of vulnerability. By allowing myself to be seen and supported, I began to find the strength to change and to begin healing. The work was far from over, but I was no longer facing it alone. By the time I reached my mid-thirties, I was drowning in self-doubt and struggling with feelings of inadequacy. In my marriage, I constantly felt lesser than, convinced that I was unworthy of love and respect. My husband, whom I placed on a pedestal, seemed to embody everything I was not. This dynamic created a significant imbalance in our relationship, where I felt perpetually inferior and insecure.

Chapter 9 Shifting Sands

Overcoming these challenges was not quick or easy. It required a lot of introspection and a willingness to confront my deepest fears. I started to equip myself with tools to manage and eventually overcome my fear of rejection. I learned that discipline, when done with love and consistency, doesn't equate to rejection. I began to understand that setting boundaries was an essential part of parenting and that it didn't make me a bad mother.

The seeds of transformation were planted during those years, as I started to see a different path unfolding before me. The work we engaged in awakened something deep within me, igniting a fire of inspiration and purpose. It was during this time that I felt the first stirrings of hope, the realisation that change was not only possible, but inevitable. Out of this period of introspection and growth emerged the birth of my business, a testament to the inner work I had undertaken and the path of self-discovery I had embarked upon. I lived and breathed personal development, dedicating myself wholeheartedly to uncovering the layers of conditioning and patterns that had shaped my life.

But as I delved deeper into the recesses of my psyche, a sense of fear and uncertainty began to take hold. I knew deep down that I couldn't stay with my husband forever, that our paths were diverging in ways that I couldn't ignore. Yet, the fear of rejection and abandonment held me back, tethering me to a relationship that no longer served my highest good. The cracks in our marriage began to widen, revealing the fault lines that had long lain hidden beneath the surface. Disagreements became more frequent, our once shared vision for the future now diverging into separate paths. At the heart of our discord lay a fundamental imbalance, a sense of inequality that permeated every aspect of our relationship.

With each passing day, I found myself growing stronger, gathering the courage to speak my truth and reclaim my sense of self-worth. I refused to continue rejecting myself, to compromise my values and desires for the sake of maintaining an illusion of harmony. It was a path of empowerment, a reclaiming of my voice and my agency in a marriage that no longer reflected who I was becoming. This realization was nothing short of extraordinary. It opened up a new world of possibilities for me, one where I had the power to change my life and my mindset.

Self-Assessment Questions

Have you ever reached a breaking point where unspoken pain and unresolved trauma became overwhelming? How did this turning point lead you to seek healing and reconnect with yourself and your loved ones?

Have you ever taken the courageous step to seek professional help for your emotional struggles?

How did the experience of being validated and supported in therapy impact your journey toward healing and self-acceptance?

Have you ever turned to a particular activity, like shopping, drinking, to cope with feelings of isolation and loneliness? How did this behaviour affect you in the long run, and what steps have you taken to address the underlying issues and find healthier ways to manage your emotions?

Chapter 10

Meeting Myself

Meeting my biological sister at 39 was one of those moments that really shifted my life in a big way. It was a rollercoaster of emotions, and I found myself grappling with so much at once. The journey to that point began back in my mid-30s when I had to finally face the hard truth—my biological mum didn't want anything to do with me. After years of trying to build some kind of relationship with her, it became painfully clear that I was banging my head against a brick wall.

She had mentioned in a letter that I had sisters, and that bit of news became my new focus. If I couldn't have a connection with her, maybe I could find it with them. It felt like a lifeline, something to hold onto when everything else seemed to be slipping away. I wasn't sure what to expect, but I knew I had to try.

There's something really confronting about realising that the person who brought you into the world doesn't want to be a part of your life. It shakes you to your core. But at the same time, it forced me to look elsewhere for that sense of belonging I'd been craving. My mum's rejection was a

Chapter 10   Meeting Myself

massive blow, but knowing I had sisters out there gave me a new direction, a new hope.

The idea of having sisters was both exciting and terrifying. I mean, how do you even begin to reach out to someone you've never met but are supposed to share this deep, biological bond with? I spent a lot of time thinking about what they might be like, whether they even knew I existed, and how they'd react to me suddenly showing up in their lives. There were so many unknowns, and I was scared of being rejected all over again.

But despite the fear, I knew I couldn't just sit back and do nothing. So, I started the search. Armed with the scraps of information from my biological mother's letter, I turned to the phonebook. It felt like a total long shot, but I was determined to give it a go. I had a few names, a unique surname she'd gone back to after a brief marriage, and a lot of hope. I figured, why not try? What did I have to lose?

The first call I made was answered by a woman who, to my surprise, actually knew my biological mother. She was connected to the family somehow—a partner of a relative, though the details were a bit fuzzy. But what stood out to me was how kind and understanding she was. She didn't rush me off the phone or make me feel like I was intruding. Instead, she let me talk, really listened, and made space for me to share my story. For someone who'd spent so long feeling like a bit of an outsider, that meant the world to me.

She confirmed that she knew of me, but there was a catch—no one else in the family did. My biological mother had kept my existence a secret all these years. That was a hard pill to swallow. I had always known on some level that I was hidden away, but hearing it confirmed by someone who was part of that world was another thing altogether. It made everything feel even more complicated.

Even so, I continued my search. There were only about nine listings with the same surname, and on my second call, I struck gold. It was my sister. Initially, she was in shock. Our (her) grandmother had recently passed away, and she feared I might be seeking money. The conversation was short and tense, but it planted a seed. Over time, we began to communicate more through messages and emails.

Within six months, we arranged to meet. I was planning a trip back to New Zealand to see my adoptive parents, and she agreed to meet me in Hawke's Bay. We chose a cafe in Clifton Beach for our first meeting. Seeing her for the first time was overwhelming. She looked like me, and I just wanted to reach out and touch her. It was an incredibly emotional experience, meeting a blood relative for the first time.

Our lunch was a rollercoaster of emotions. We talked, laughed, and I cried—more than once. There was something about finally sitting across from my sister, this person who was a part of me yet so foreign, that stirred up feelings I didn't even know I had. When she left, I remember feeling this intense longing for her to stay, like I was losing something all over again. We met up the next day, but that ended up being the last time. She had a deep sense of loyalty to her mother and just couldn't continue our relationship. It hurt—a lot—but over time, I've come to accept her decision. Back then, it was devastating. Now, I'm at peace with it.

Even though things didn't pan out as I'd hoped with my sister, I couldn't shake the need to understand where I came from. By the time I hit my late 40s, that curiosity had only grown stronger. So, I decided to track down my biological father. The adoption agency had his name, but because he wasn't listed on my birth certificate, it wasn't simple. I basically had two options: petition to change the adoption act to get his name released or, once again, reach out to my biological mother.

Changing the adoption act felt like a massive mountain to climb, and honestly, I wasn't sure I had the energy for that kind of battle. That's when my youngest son piped up with some simple but solid advice: "You always taught us to ask questions," he said. It was one of those moments where your own words come back to you, and I realized he was right. Instead of jumping through a million legal hoops, I could just ask her. So, I took a deep breath and decided to give it one more shot.

Summoning all the courage I had, I picked up the phone and called my biological mother. I wasn't sure if she'd answer or if she'd hang up as soon as she heard my voice, but to my surprise, she picked up. Our conversation was brief, just two minutes, but she provided his details without any hesitation. It was so matter-of-fact that it caught me off guard. After I hung up, I just sat there, phone in hand, and silently wept. I cried for what was, for what is, and for that fleeting moment in time when our lives intersected again. I wept for the woman who birthed me, who didn't want me then and still didn't want me now, and for the cold, hard reality of it all.

With the information she gave me, I dove headfirst into the search for my biological father. For a couple of years, I scoured records in both Australia and New Zealand, hoping to find a trace of him. But it was like he had vanished into thin air. I knew he was of Scottish descent, so there was always the possibility that he had returned there, but even that lead didn't get me anywhere. After a while, I had to face the fact that this might be a part of my history that would forever remain a mystery. It was a hard pill to swallow, but eventually, I made peace with the idea that some things are just meant to stay hidden.

Reflecting on these experiences, I realize how they shaped my understanding of identity and belonging. Each step of the way, from my initial search for my mother to meeting my sister and finally seeking my father, has been a process of self-discovery. It taught me resilience, the importance of asking questions, and ultimately, the need to accept what cannot be changed. These relationships, or the lack thereof, have influenced how I see myself and my place in the world. Though the answers weren't always what I hoped for, the process itself was invaluable. It allowed me to confront my feelings of abandonment and rejection, and to find a measure of peace within myself. My story, like many adoptees', is one of searching for connection, understanding, and acceptance.

In my late 30s, I discovered a transformative workshop that offered a series of programs designed to help men and women heal from deep-seated traumas. Intrigued by the potential for healing, I shared this with my husband. Surprisingly, he agreed to attend the Thursday-through-Sunday workshop. This was the beginning of a joint two year commitment of self-exploration. It was a life changing experience for both of us. Our relationship had always been founded on mutual trauma. He carried significant wounds from his past, and so did I. We existed in a shared space of pain, often drowning in our unresolved issues. Our communication was poor, and I had placed him on a pedestal, which left me feeling perpetually lesser than. This dynamic, this trauma bond was unhealthy and unsustainable.

This individual therapy was crucial, but the workshop experience added another dimension to my healing process. It pushed us to confront our deepest wounds—the father wounds, the mother wounds, and all the complex emotions tied to them. These workshops were experimental and intense, demanding us to look inward and examine the foundations of our pain. This period of self-exploration and healing marked a significant shift in our relationship. As I grew stronger, building confidence and self-esteem, the dynamics between us began to change. No longer did I see my husband as a figure to be idolized. I started to see him as an equal, which altered the balance of our relationship. This newfound equality and my rising self-assurance led to increasing tension between us.

I came to the understanding that our relationship might not withstand the changes I was undergoing. I was evolving, shedding old beliefs and patterns that had kept me subservient and insecure. As I grew, our communication issues became more apparent. The cracks in our relationship widened as I refused to return to the dynamics of our past. My husband didn't seem to appreciate the new me. As I gained confidence, our clashes became more frequent. Our inability to communicate effectively exacerbated these conflicts. I was no longer willing to stay silent or accept being treated as lesser than. This shift was liberating for me, but it was also the beginning of the end for our marriage.

I understand now that our relationship was a mirror for our traumas. We were drawn to each other because of our unresolved issues, and we stayed together out of a mutual need to avoid confronting our pain. But healing requires confrontation and courage. As I confronted my past and worked to heal my wounds, the relationship that was built on those wounds inevitably started to crumble. The workshop and subsequent counselling were critical in this process. They provided the tools and insights needed to understand the roots of my behaviour and beliefs. Through these experiences, I learned that healing is ongoing. It's about peeling back the layers, understanding the origins of our pain, and finding healthier ways to navigate relationships.

In the end, my decision to focus on my healing, even at the cost of my marriage, was the right one. It allowed me to break free from the cycles of trauma that had defined my life and relationships. This period of intense self-discovery and growth was painful but necessary. It paved the way for a future where I could build relationships based on mutual respect and healthy communication, rather than shared trauma and unspoken pain.

I was nearly 40 and deeply entrenched in self-discovery and healing. The therapy and workshops I had participated in were peeling back layers of my past, exposing the raw wounds and buried traumas that had shaped my life. This transformative process was difficult, but it also sparked a knowing within me: I wanted to help others heal. This was not just a fleeting thought—it felt like a calling, a soul's purpose. I had spent years dabbling in self-help and therapy, and I had seen the benefits firsthand. Now, I wanted to share these benefits with others. I envisioned myself working with adoptees, helping them navigate the complex emotions and challenges that come with being adopted. I wanted to be a beacon of hope and healing, guiding others through the darkness that I had once experienced as I had desperately needed.

This calling was completely driven by my own inner work. As I worked through my issues, I began to feel lighter. The constant ache in my heart started to ease, and the emptiness that had once consumed me began to fill with hope and light. If I could find healing and joy after years of pain, then perhaps I could help others do the same. However, I quickly learned that not all adoptees were ready to confront their pasts. Many were reluctant to delve into the pain and trauma associated with their adoption. This realization forced me to broaden my approach. I decided to offer more mainstream coaching and counselling services, expanding my reach and helping a wider range of people.

My decision to become a counsellor and healer was rooted in a deep, intrinsic knowing. It was as if my soul had always known this was my path. The work I had done on myself—continued to do on myself, learning self-care, and building self-trust—had prepared me for this role. I had spent much of my life prioritizing others' needs over my own, always seeking external validation. But as I learned to care for myself, I also learned to trust myself. This newfound trust became the foundation of my work as a counsellor.

Healing in Practice

Trust is a critical issue for many people and adoptees. The interruption of trust that occurs when a child is placed for adoption can leave deep scars. For years, I had struggled with trust—trusting others and trusting myself. But as I began to look inward, I learned to trust my instincts and my capacity for self-care. This was a monumental shift for me. For the first time, I wasn't looking to others for validation or approval. I was looking within.

This was an unravelling of old beliefs and patterns. It was about peeling back the layers of my past and understanding how they had shaped my present. It was about learning to put myself first, something that had always been foreign to me. My entire existence had been about meeting others' needs, making sure they were happy so that I could feel secure. But as I learned to care for myself, I discovered a new kind of security—one that came from within.

My path to becoming a counsellor and coach was not straightforward. It was a winding road filled with challenges and revelations. But every step of the way, I felt guided by an inner knowing that this was what I was meant to do. Helping others heal became my purpose, my mission. And in helping others, I continued to heal myself. I can look back now on those early years and be grateful for the struggles and the pain, for they led me to my true calling. Becoming a counsellor was more than a career choice; it was the fulfillment of my soul's purpose. And in embracing this purpose, I found a sense of peace and fulfillment that I had never known before.

I also had another equally important goal: learning to take care of myself. This was a foreign concept to me, as my entire life had been spent prioritizing the needs of others over my own. However, through intensive counselling and daily practices, I began to establish a relationship with myself, one built on self-awareness and self-care.

Understanding the beliefs we hold about ourselves is crucial in shaping how we approach self-care. Often, deep-seated, limiting beliefs like "I can't put my needs first" or "I'm not important" can drive us to neglect our well-being, leading to burnout, stress, and a lack of balance in our lives.

These beliefs, often rooted in past experiences or societal expectations, can trap us in cycles of self-neglect, where taking care of ourselves feels like an indulgence rather than a necessity. However, by recognising and challenging these limiting beliefs, we can begin to embrace more empowering perspectives, such as "I am allowed to honour my needs first" or "I am worthy regardless of my achievements." Shifting these beliefs is not just about changing your mindset but also about creating a foundation for consistent, meaningful self-care that supports your overall health and happiness.

Five Limiting Sabotaging Beliefs in the Context of Self-Care

"I can't put my needs first"
- Impact on Self-Care: If you believe that prioritising your own needs is selfish, you're likely to neglect self-care. This belief can lead to burnout as you constantly put others' needs ahead of your own, leaving little time or energy to look after yourself.

"I don't fit in"
- Impact on Self-Care: Feeling like you don't belong can isolate you and make it hard to seek support or engage in social activities that contribute to your well-being. This belief might cause you to withdraw, avoiding group activities that could boost your mental and emotional health.

"I'm not important"

- Impact on Self-Care: When you think you're not important, you may struggle to see the value in taking care of yourself. This belief can result in neglecting your health, both physically and emotionally, as you might feel your well-being isn't worth the effort.

"I'm damaged goods"

- Impact on Self-Care: Believing that you're damaged can lead to feelings of unworthiness, making it difficult to engage in self-care. You might feel that you don't deserve kindness or care, leading to self-sabotage or neglecting activities that promote healing and self-compassion.

"I need to prove my worth by achieving"

- Impact on Self-Care: This belief can push you to constantly strive for success, often at the expense of your health. You might prioritise work or achievements over rest and relaxation, leading to stress, exhaustion, and a lack of balance in your life.

Opposite Empowering Beliefs in the Context of Self-Care

"I can put my needs first"

- Impact on Self-Care: Embracing this belief allows you to prioritise self-care without guilt. You recognise that looking after yourself is essential for your well-being, enabling you to recharge and be more effective in supporting others.

"I belong"
- Impact on Self-Care: When you believe you belong, you're more likely to engage in social activities and seek support from others. This sense of connection fosters a community where self-care can thrive, as you feel supported and valued by those around you.

"I am important"
- Impact on Self-Care: Acknowledging your importance empowers you to invest in self-care. You see the value in looking after your health and well-being, understanding that you deserve to feel good and that your happiness matters.

"I am whole"
- Impact on Self-Care: Believing that you're whole and not broken encourages self-compassion and healing. You focus on nurturing yourself, recognising that you have the strength and resilience to grow from past experiences and prioritise your well-being.

"I am worthy no matter what I achieve"
- Impact on Self-Care: This belief helps you to separate your worth from your accomplishments, allowing you to take breaks, rest, and enjoy life without the constant pressure to achieve. You understand that self-care is essential and that your value isn't tied to how much you do, but simply to who you are.

Self-Assessment Questions

What is the strongest self-sabotaging belief you still live with, and why do you think it continues to hold power over you?

Have you ever felt a deep yearning to understand your origins or past? How did you navigate the challenges of seeking out this information, and what role did your loved ones play in encouraging and supporting your journey?

Have you ever been in a relationship where mutual trauma influenced your connection? How did the unresolved issues and poor communication impact your self-esteem, and what steps did you take to address the unhealthy dynamic?

Chapter 11

Giving Out Instead of Giving In

When we were trying to sell our property, things really started to fall apart. For seven frustrating years, our acreage just wouldn't budge, even after six different buyers had a go at it. The stress of keeping up with the property, my ex-husband's health issues, and raising teenagers was almost too much to bear. It all piled up, creating this massive wave of resentment and overwhelm that nearly swallowed me whole. With everything going on, the cracks in our marriage were becoming impossible to ignore.

But, my 40s weren't just about struggle—they were also about serious growth and change. Year by year, I started to really step into my own, finding my voice and standing up for what I needed in our relationship. But as I became stronger and more certain of my own path, the tension and conflicts in our marriage ramped up even more.

In those heated moments, my husband's words felt like daggers, slicing through old wounds and reigniting the fears of rejection and abandonment that had haunted me for years. His dismissive tone and harsh ultimatums didn't just hurt— they sent me spiralling into a deeper sense of loneliness and despair. The more we argued, the more isolated I felt, and the more the weight of our crumbling marriage pressed down on me. It was like living in a pressure cooker, with the lid about to blow at any second.

I could feel myself being pulled back into those old, destructive patterns of co-dependency and avoidance. The urge to run, to escape the pain rather than face it, was overwhelming. I was caught in this cycle, knowing something had to give, but too paralysed to make a move. I was stuck, teetering on the edge of a cliff, unsure whether to leap or fall back into the same old web.

I was stuck.

As a committed runner, I'd always turned to physical exercise as my go-to for stress relief and emotional release. Running was my sanctuary, a way to clear my mind and recharge my spirit. But as adrenal fatigue took its toll, even the simple act of lacing up my runners became a daunting task. What had once been a source of peace and strength now felt like an impossible challenge, leaving me even more drained and worn out. The exhaustion was all-encompassing, and the very thing that used to bring me balance was now tipping me further into depletion.

During this, I realized that I needed a different kind of refuge, one that didn't demand physical exertion but offered a deeper form of healing. I'd toyed with meditation on and off over the years, but it wasn't until I hit my mid-forties, faced with the reality of my burnout, that I truly embraced its power.

Meditation became my new sanctuary, a quiet, sacred space where I could escape the whirlwind of daily life and reconnect with the core of who I was.

Through meditation, I found a stillness that running could no longer provide. It offered me a way to soothe my frazzled nerves and replenish my depleted energy reserves. More importantly, it gave me the tools to listen to my body and mind in a way I never had before. In that quiet space, I began to repair—not just physically, but emotionally and spiritually as well.

As the demands of motherhood and family life escalated, I found myself sinking into a relentless cycle of exhaustion and chaos. Juggling the needs of three growing sons, working, managing the household, and trying to keep some semblance of peace in my relationship was pushing me to my limits, both physically and emotionally. Little by little, my body started sending me warning signals in the form of strange health symptoms that left me feeling utterly wiped out. It was like my body was waving a red flag, trying to tell me that something was seriously off.

Looking back, I can now see that these were classic signs of adrenal fatigue. My adrenal glands, worn out from constant stress, were no longer able to keep up. The most obvious clue was the sudden onset of flu-like symptoms—body aches, a deep-seated fatigue, and a general feeling of being unwell. I was constantly tired, like someone had drained every bit of energy from me. Even the simplest tasks felt overwhelming, as if just getting through the day was a monumental effort.

Chapter 11   Giving Out Instead of Giving In

These symptoms were more than just physical; they were a wake-up call. My body was clearly telling me that I couldn't keep going the way I was. It was a moment of reckoning, forcing me to face the reality that I needed to take better care of myself before I could take care of anyone else.

I had already made the decision to dive into the world of coaching, drawn by the idea of helping others unlock their potential and overcome life's hurdles. Coaching gave me a fresh perspective on how powerful intentionality can be, and it opened my eyes to the ways we can shape our own lives. But as I got deeper into it, I started to realise that if I really wanted to help people make lasting changes, I needed to go beyond the surface. There was a whole world beneath, in the deeper layers of the human mind, that I was only beginning to understand.

This realisation is what pushed me towards mainstream counselling training. I wanted to get to the root of human behaviour, to understand the psychological mechanisms that drive us and shape our actions. Through my counselling training, I gained a solid grounding in therapeutic techniques and principles. I learned how to truly listen, to facilitate healing, and to navigate the complex terrain of the human psyche. It was in this space that I found a new level of understanding—not just for others, but for myself as well.

Yet, there was still a part of me that yearned for a more holistic approach—one that respected the deep connection between mind, body, and spirit. This desire nudged me towards holistic counselling, where I began to weave together traditional therapeutic methods with holistic and spiritual principles. I ventured into the realms of hypnotherapy and psychotherapy, learning just how much the subconscious mind influences our thoughts, emotions, and behaviours.

Through hypnotherapy, I uncovered a powerful way to reach deep into the psyche, accessing and healing traumas and ingrained patterns that had been holding clients back for years. It became clear to me that true transformation happens from the inside out, and with this approach, I could guide clients in reshaping their lives on a much deeper level. The combination of mainstream counselling with holistic practices offered a more complete pathway to healing, one that could honour all aspects of a person's being.

Throughout my training and practice, I stayed dedicated to my own personal growth and rebuilding. I knew that to be an effective counsellor, I couldn't just be a "wounded healer"—I needed to be someone who had faced their own pain and come out stronger on the other side. I understood that my own healing journey wasn't just for me; it was crucial for the work I did with others.

Being a healer meant I had to confront my own unhealed wounds and the shadows they cast. It required acknowledging them, seeking out support when I needed it, and never shying away from the tough stuff. I had to stay open and vulnerable, even when my clients brought their deepest struggles into our sessions. It meant embracing my humanity and imperfections while holding space for others to do the same.

Beneath the surface of this adrenaline-fueled existence lay a deeper, more insidious belief that happiness was contingent upon external achievement and validation. I convinced myself that I would only find true fulfillment once I had it all—success, recognition, and material abundance. Little did I realize that true wealth resides not in the accumulation of possessions, but in the cultivation of inner harmony and self-awareness. It wasn't until I embarked on a pathway of holistic healing and self-discovery that I began to unravel the layers of conditioning and beliefs that had kept me trapped in a cycle of self-neglect and striving. Through my exploration of alternative therapies and holistic modalities, I encountered a shift that urged me to slow down, to listen to the whispers of my body, and to reconnect with the wisdom that lay dormant within.

I still grappled with the complexities of my relationship dynamics. The patterns of communication within my partnership were marked by an imbalance, characterized by my tendency to defer to my partner's needs and desires at the expense of my own.

Healing in Practice

In my work as a holistic healer, I strive to embody the principles of head, heart, and gut—an integrated approach that honours the complexity of human experience. I reject the notion of treating symptoms in isolation, recognizing that true healing requires addressing the root causes of suffering and restoring balance to the whole being. As I continue on this road of self-discovery and service, I remain committed to expanding my knowledge, refining my skills, and deepening my understanding of what it means to be a healer. Each day brings new opportunities for growth and learning, and I am grateful for the privilege of accompanying others on their path to wholeness and transformation.

Trauma is often misunderstood as merely a memory—a recollection of past events that evoke emotional distress. However, the reality is far more intricate and multifaceted. Trauma is not just a mental construct; it is a physiological response deeply ingrained in the body and brain. From a psychological perspective, trauma encompasses a wide range of experiences that overwhelm an individual's capacity to cope. These experiences may include incidents where one feels unseen, unheard, invalidated, or isolated. Even seemingly minor events, such as the loss of a beloved pet, can have effects on a developing psyche if not adequately processed and integrated.

Imagine a child grieving the death of their dog. It is an experience that elicits raw emotions of sadness, anger, and confusion. In an ideal scenario, the child would receive comfort and support from nurturing caregivers who validate their feelings and help them navigate through the grieving process. However, for many individuals, especially those raised in environments lacking in emotional attunement and support, such experiences may be met with dismissal or indifference. In such instances, the child learns to suppress their emotions as a means of self-preservation. They internalize the message that their feelings are not valid or worthy of acknowledgment, leading to a pattern of emotional avoidance and dissociation. This survival strategy becomes deeply ingrained, shaping their response to future stressors and challenges and relationships.

For individuals like me, who grew up in environments marked by neglect or emotional turmoil, the process of trauma processing is fraught with complexities. During childhood, the focus is on survival—meeting basic needs and navigating volatile family dynamics. There is little room for emotional expression or processing, as the priority is simply to endure.

As I entered adulthood, the unresolved trauma of my childhood began to manifest in various ways, including panic attacks, anxiety and overwhelming emotional triggers. These experiences served as poignant reminders of the unhealed wounds lurking beneath the surface, demanding attention and resolution. Through years of introspection, therapy, coaching and self-care, I have gradually unravelled the layers of my trauma, confronting painful memories and challenging belief systems. Yet, even now, decades later, I still encounter triggers that transport me back to moments of vulnerability and distress. What is different today is I have awareness and can recognise what I'm feeling in my body and allow it to be here. Sadness is visiting, or guilt is here. I can name it and allow it to visit and sometimes explore where's this coming from? The crucial ingredient is the love, the nurturing I can give myself. No longer looking outside of myself I can give myself the unconditional love I've been searching for my entire life.

From a neurological standpoint, trauma leaves an indelible imprint on the brain, reshaping neural pathways and influencing cognitive and emotional processing. The amygdala, the brain's fear centre, becomes hyperactive, triggering the body's fight-flight-freeze response in seemingly benign situations. Moreover, trauma can impair the prefrontal cortex, compromising executive functions such as impulse control, decision-making, and emotional regulation. Understanding trauma as more than just a memory is essential for cultivating empathy and compassion towards individuals navigating the complex terrain of healing. It is a reflective journey of self-discovery and integration, where past wounds intersect with present realities, shaping our perceptions, behaviours, and relationships.

In seeking guidance and support, I turned to many professionals who played a pivotal role in identifying and addressing the underlying root cause of my symptoms. Through a combination of holistic modalities, including regular massages, meditation, and dietary adjustments, I began to reclaim a sense of balance and vitality that had long eluded me. However, the way toward healing was not without its challenges. It required a fundamental shift in mindset—a willingness to prioritize self-care and cultivate a deeper sense of compassion and nurturance toward myself. To have awareness when the high achiever in me is obsessive and overachieving. The inner wealth I sought was the awareness of my feelings and thoughts, acceptance

Chapter 11   Giving Out Instead of Giving In

of my present reality, and the authentic action necessary for change.

In the pursuit of inner wealth, I found myself locked in a perpetual battle—a relentless struggle against my own instincts and inner wisdom. For close to a decade, I grappled with a myriad of health symptoms that left me feeling depleted and exhausted, yet I chose to fight against the whispers of my body, drowning out its cries for attention with the cacophony of my own beliefs and desires. It's remarkable to reflect on the extent to which I allowed myself to be ensnared by beliefs that ultimately hindered my well-being. One such belief was my addiction to adrenaline—a relentless craving for the rush of excitement and intensity that fuelled my existence. In my relentless pursuit of achievement and success, I became addicted to the thrill of the chase, pushing myself to the brink of exhaustion in search of fleeting moments of fulfillment. This is the mouse wheel that many high achievers get trapped on and swept up in including myself.

Self-Assessment Questions

How has your journey of self-discovery influenced your understanding of trauma? What insights have you gained about trauma, and how has this shaped your approach to helping others heal?

Have you ever felt the need to suppress your emotions to protect yourself? How has this pattern affected your response to stress and challenges, and what steps have you taken to acknowledge and address your feelings?

Have you ever experienced physical and emotional exhaustion from the demands of daily life? How did your body signal that something was wrong, and what steps did you take to address your health and well-being?

Chapter 12

Mother and Marriage

Life has a way of delivering intense changes when we least expect them, shaking the very foundations of our existence and forcing us to confront the uncomfortable truths that lie beneath the surface. For me, the year of my 49th birthday marked the beginning of a tumultuous period of transition—a time of loss, grief, and ultimately, rebirth. In the span of just a few short months, my world was upended in ways I could never have imagined. The end of my 30-year marriage/relationship came swiftly and decisively, leaving me reeling with the shock and devastation of its sudden demise. There were no marriage counselling sessions, no attempts at reconciliation—just the cold, hard reality of a relationship that had run its course.

As November rolled around, I found myself at a crossroads. Sitting at the bar with my husband, the weight of my decision hung heavy in the air as I mustered the courage to speak my truth. It was a conversation I had mulled over for years, a decision I had wrestled with in the depths of my soul. And yet, in that moment, as I looked into his eyes, I knew with unwavering certainty that it was time to reclaim my power.

With a deep breath, I spoke the words that had long lingered unspoken, setting in motion a series of events that would irrevocably alter the course of my life.

"I want you to get your physical needs met elsewhere" I declared, the words echoing in the space between us with a weighty finality. It was a declaration of independence, a reclaiming of my autonomy over my body, and a refusal to continue sacrificing my own well-being for the sake of a relationship that no longer served me. He didn't argue.

Separation can feel like a deep, unrelenting grief—the kind that takes your breath away and leaves a void in your chest that nothing seems to fill. It's not just the end of a relationship; it's the death of a promise, a shared future that once seemed so certain. The vows exchanged, the dreams built together, the life you envisioned—all of it crumbles, leaving behind the rubble of what was supposed to be.

For years, I held on, clinging to the remnants of our marriage, not because I believed in a future together, but because of two powerful forces: my kids and my fear of failure. The thought of breaking up our family was a weight I couldn't bear. The idea of being alone, of facing the world without the safety net of my marriage, terrified me. I was afraid of what it would mean for my children, for their sense of stability and security. I was afraid of what it would mean for me—what people would think, how I would cope, and whether I was strong enough to stand on my own.

When you have kids, every decision feels like it's under a

microscope. You want to do right by them, to make sure they have the best possible upbringing, and sometimes that leads you to make choices that aren't necessarily the best for you. I told myself that staying in the marriage was for their sake, that it was better for them to have two parents under one roof, even if that roof was under constant strain. I convinced myself that stability meant continuity, even if that continuity was marred by tension, arguments, and a palpable unhappiness that seeped into every corner of our home.

But children are perceptive. They pick up on the unspoken, on the tension that lingers in the air, on the way their parents avoid each other's gaze or speak in clipped tones. I started to realize that holding on for the kids wasn't doing them any favours. It wasn't giving them the healthy, loving environment they deserved. Instead, it was teaching them that love looks like endurance, that relationships are about survival rather than connection. I began to see that the longer I stayed, the more I was modelling a version of marriage that I didn't want for them—a marriage that was more about cohabitation than companionship, more about duty than joy.

Beyond the kids, there was the gnawing fear of failure that kept me tethered to the relationship. I had always prided myself on being capable, on holding it all together no matter what life threw my way. The thought of a failed marriage felt like a personal failing, a glaring flaw in the carefully constructed image I had of myself. I was scared of what others would think—friends, family, society. I didn't want to be seen as someone who couldn't make it work, who had somehow failed at one of life's most important endeavours.

But the fear ran deeper than just external perceptions. It was also about what it meant to me. I had invested so much of myself into this marriage—my time, my energy, my love. To walk away felt like admitting that all of that effort had been for nothing, that I had wasted years of my life chasing something that was never meant to be. It was hard to let go of the future we had planned together, even if that future no longer seemed possible. There was a deep sense of loss, not just of the relationship, but of the person I had been in that relationship.

And then there was the fear of being alone. The idea of starting over, of facing the world as a single woman, was daunting. I had been with my husband for so long that I couldn't imagine life without him, even if our relationship was no longer fulfilling. I was scared of the loneliness, of the quiet nights and empty weekends, of not having someone to share my life with. I was scared of the unknown, of stepping into a new chapter without knowing what it would hold.

But deep down, I knew that staying in the marriage out of fear wasn't sustainable. The longer I stayed, the more the fear grew, feeding on itself until it felt like a cage, trapping me in a life that no longer felt like my own. I was holding on to something that was already gone, trying to keep alive a relationship that had long since lost its pulse. It was like trying to resuscitate a body that had no life left in it, refusing to accept that it was time to let go.

Chapter 12 Mother and Marriage

Separation really is a form of grief. It's the mourning of a relationship, the death of the love you once had, the dreams you shared, and the life you built together. It's the loss of the person you thought you knew, of the future you thought was certain. Just like any other form of grief, it comes with stages—denial, anger, bargaining, depression, and, eventually, acceptance. But unlike other forms of grief, this one is complicated by the fact that the person you're grieving is still alive, still there, still a part of your life in some way, especially when you have kids together.

The grief of separation is also layered with guilt and self-doubt. You question whether you did enough, whether you could have saved the marriage if you had just tried a little harder, held on a little longer. You wonder if you're making the right choice, if you're sacrificing too much or giving up too soon. It's a grief that's intertwined with fear—the fear of the unknown, of what comes next, of whether you'll ever find love again, or if you'll end up alone.

When we get married, we make a promise—to love, to cherish, to honour, in sickness and in health, for better or worse. It's a promise that we believe in, that we hold onto, even when things get tough. But sometimes, despite our best efforts, that promise is broken. It's not always one person's fault—sometimes, it's just life. People change, circumstances change, and what once worked no longer does. The promise of love is beautiful, but it's not always enough to sustain a relationship.

The hardest part about separation is letting go of that

promise, of accepting that the love you once had has changed or faded or been lost along the way. It's acknowledging that the relationship has run its course, that it's time to let go, even if you're not ready to. It's coming to terms with the fact that sometimes, love isn't enough to keep a marriage together.

Ultimately, I realized that holding on out of fear wasn't fair to anyone—not to my kids, not to my husband, and certainly not to myself. I had to face the reality that staying in a marriage that was no longer working was causing more harm than good. Letting go was terrifying, but it was also liberating. It was a chance to start over, to redefine myself, to find out who I was outside of the marriage. It was an opportunity to create a new life, one that was more in line with my values, my desires, and my true self.

As I grappled with the pain of separation and the uncertainty of the future, I found myself navigating a landscape of loss. My mother's passing, mere months earlier, had left a void in my life that seemed impossible to fill and a grief compounded by the end of my marriage and the departure of my middle son from the family home. I made the difficult decision for myself leave the family home that had been the backdrop to so many cherished memories. It was the place where my children had grown and thrived, and where I had built a life with my former husband. Moving out was a bittersweet experience, marked by loss and nostalgia for the life I was leaving behind. Once again, I was untethered.

Chapter 12 Mother and Marriage

Even though our relationship had always been rocky, my mother's death hit me hard. It shattered the fragile facade we'd built around our strained connection and forced me to confront the sadness and introspection I'd been avoiding for years. Mum and I had always had a complicated relationship, full of tension and unspoken truths. We danced around each other, both avoiding the real issues but still craving a connection that always felt just out of reach. I spent years feeling like I was hiding parts of myself, terrified that if I showed her the real me, she'd somehow violate the safety of my inner world. Our chats were always pretty surface-level, avoiding the big stuff and keeping my deeper feelings well out of sight.

In the final weeks before her passing, there was a glimmer of intimacy—a fleeting glimpse of the bond that had eluded us for so long. I remember sitting by her bedside, our words laden with softened emotion as we gently shared and chatted and enjoyed our time together. It was a moment of vulnerability, a glimpse into the depths of our shared humanity that transcended the barriers of pain and regret. And then, a few weeks later with heartbreaking swiftness, she was gone.

After Mum passed, I was hit by a wave of grief that felt like it could swallow me whole. It was a whirlwind of emotions—so intense and overwhelming that I had no choice but to retreat into myself. I found some sense of calm in the quiet moments alone, away from the world, as I tried to wrap my head around the magnitude of the loss.

As a counsellor, I knew how crucial it was to let myself

fully feel and process every emotion, no matter how gut-wrenching it was. I wasn't about to skip over the pain or push it aside. I knew that to truly heal, I had to face the grief head-on. It wasn't easy, but I understood that avoiding the pain would only prolong the suffering. So, I sat with it, allowed it to wash over me, and slowly began the process of piecing myself back together.

I let myself surrender completely to the waves of grief, allowing them to pull me under so I could truly wade through the murky depths of my sorrow. It was a painful process, but it felt necessary—like I had to go through it to come out the other side. I found comfort in creating small rituals of remembrance and reflection, ways to honour Mum's memory while also facing the complicated reality of our relationship.

Through moments of tears, bursts of laughter, flashes of anger, and finally, some level of acceptance, I began to untangle the messy threads of our shared history. It wasn't always easy, but in that process, I realised that our connection, complicated as it was, still endured, even after she was gone. It wasn't just about her being gone; it was about the connection I'd always longed for but never quite found. I'd spent so much of my life hoping, wishing, and longing for that bond, for her to truly see me and understand me.

For me, Mum represented more than just a mother. She was a symbol of everything I felt was missing in my life, a vessel for all the hopes and dreams I'd never been able to voice. But no matter how much I tried, our relationship always seemed

Chapter 12   Mother and Marriage

tangled in a web of silent truths and unresolved feelings. I wanted so desperately to connect with her in a way that went beyond just being mother and daughter, to build a bond that was deeper, more meaningful. But that gap between us always felt insurmountable.

This grief was layered with the complexities of adoption, too—a grief not just for the mother I lost, but for the mother I never truly got to know. It was a mourning for the childhood that felt incomplete, for the unanswered questions that still lingered, and for that elusive sense of belonging that always seemed just out of reach.

I discovered a resilience I didn't know I had—a strength that came from embracing my vulnerability and a kind of wisdom that was only possible through the fires of loss. It was in those moments of deep sorrow that I found a way to rebuild myself, piece by piece, emerging with a deeper understanding of both myself and the bond I had with my mother.

And yet, amidst the pain and the longing, there was also a glimmer of understanding and a recognition that our relationship, however imperfect, was still a source of connection. In the quiet moments of reflection, I found comfort in the knowledge that even in death, our bond endured and it was a testament to the enduring power of love and resilience. As I navigated the complex terrain of adoption and maternal grief, I was reminded that healing is not always linear. It was okay to mourn the relationship we never had. In the end, it is our ability to embrace the full spectrum of our emotions—to honour the pain even as we embrace the peace—that allows us to move forward.

I returned to my soul's home, where the comfort of nature wrapped around me like a warm hug. In the peaceful sanctuary of a wooded glen behind my new place, I found solace among the trees. The ancient wisdom of the bush and the gentle rustle of leaves in the breeze offered me a quiet refuge. There, surrounded by nature's silent sentinels, I allowed myself the space to grieve, to mourn the losses that weighed heavy on my heart, and to make peace with what lay ahead.

Grief, I realised, is an intense and winding path with unexpected detours and moments of quiet grace. Each morning, I let myself sink deep into the sorrow, fully embracing the pain that pulsed through me. I knew I had to honour the losses I'd endured, to acknowledge their weight before I could start to heal. But I also knew I needed balance. In the evenings, I sought comfort in the simple joys of life—a glass of red wine, the soft glow of a Netflix binge, and the empowering stories of strong women who had faced their own storms and come out the other side with grace and resilience. These small acts of self-care became my lifeline, a way to nurture myself as I navigated the turbulent waters of grief. Little did I know there was more to come.

Healing in Practice

The intricacies of the mother-daughter bond are woven with threads of love, understanding, and shared experiences.

Chapter 12   Mother and Marriage

But for those of us touched by adoption, these threads can sometimes feel frayed, stretched thin by the weight of unsaid truths and unfulfilled expectations. As an adopted daughter, my relationship with my mother was always tinged with a sense of longing and a yearning for a connection that transcended the boundaries of biology. From a young age, I grappled with feelings of grief and confusion, haunted by the spectre of a mother I barely knew. She was a woman whose love and acceptance always seemed just out of reach

Through it all, I learned that grief is not a sign of weakness. It is a testament to the depth of our capacity to love. And as I made my way through the darkness, I emerged on the other side with a newfound sense of strength and resilience and a testament to the transformative power of embracing our pain and allowing ourselves to be transformed by it. I embarked on the road of self-healing to reclaim my sense of wholeness and rediscover the depths of my own resilience. For me, healing was not a passive endeavour—it was an active, ongoing process of self-discovery and self-care, guided by an unwavering commitment to my own well-being.

I delved into a myriad of healing modalities, each offering its own unique insights and opportunities for growth. From the transformative power of journaling to the restorative benefits of meditation, I embraced every opportunity to nurture my mind, body, and spirit. One of the cornerstones of my healing was the work of an introspective practice that invited me to challenge my deepest beliefs and question the narratives that had shaped my understanding of myself and the world around me. Through rigorous self-inquiry and compassionate self-reflection, I began to unravel the tangled threads of my own inner landscape, gaining clarity and insight into the patterns that had kept me trapped in cycles of suffering.

In addition to inner work, I also sought out external support in the form of holistic therapies and alternative healing modalities. Regular massages, acupuncture sessions provided much-needed relief for my weary body, easing tension and releasing stagnant energy stored within my muscles and tissues. And through neuro-emotional technique sessions with a skilled chiropractor, I discovered the connection between physical health and emotional well-being, as old traumas were gently released from my body, allowing for a deeper sense of healing to take place.

Yet, among the plethora of healing practices and modalities like breath work, kinesiology, family constellation, I knew that true healing could not be found in external solutions alone. It required a willingness to dive deep into the recesses of my own psyche, confronting the shadows and embracing the light with equal measure. It was self-discovery and reclaiming my power to reconnect with the essence of who I truly was. While formal counselling may not have been the right fit for me at that particular moment in time, I found strength in the knowledge that I possessed the skills and tools necessary to navigate my own healing. Through a combination of self-awareness, self-compassion, and unwavering self-love, I continued to move forward on the path of healing, trusting in the wisdom of my own inner guidance and the transformative power of my own innate resilience.

- Embrace Self-Awareness: Start by cultivating an honest awareness of your emotions, thoughts, and behaviours. Regularly check in with yourself, asking questions like, "How do I truly feel?" or "What is driving my current reaction?" This self-reflection is essential for identifying patterns and triggers that may need healing.

- Practice Self-Compassion: Treat yourself with the same kindness and understanding that you would offer a friend. When you encounter difficult emotions or memories, resist the urge to judge yourself harshly. Instead, acknowledge your feelings and remind yourself that it's okay to feel this way. Ask, "What am I feeling? Where in my body am I feeling it? What colour is it?"

- Dive Into Your Shadows: Don't shy away from the uncomfortable or painful aspects of your psyche. Confronting your shadows, those hidden parts of yourself that you may avoid or suppress, is key to deep healing. For example, the parts of yourself you see as unacceptable; sadness, rage, laziness, self-hate. Journaling, meditation, or guided visualizations can help you explore these areas with curiosity and compassion.

- Integrate Breath Work: Incorporate breath work into your daily routine to help manage stress and foster a deeper connection with your body. Simple techniques like deep belly breathing or alternate nostril breathing can bring calmness and clarity, making it easier to process emotions and thoughts.

- Explore Kinesiology and Family Constellation: These modalities can offer insights into physical and emotional blockages. While they can be powerful tools, use them as complements to your inner work rather than relying on them entirely. Allow them to guide you, but also trust your intuition.

- Cultivate Self-Love: Actively practice self-love by engaging in activities that nourish your soul, whether it's spending time in nature, engaging in creative pursuits, or simply taking time to rest. Affirm your worthiness and recognize that you deserve love and care from yourself.

- Trust Your Inner Wisdom: Listen to your inner guidance and trust your intuition. Your body and mind often know what you need to heal, even if the path isn't immediately clear. Allow your inner voice to lead you towards practices and choices that feel right for you.

- Reclaim Your Power: Recognize that true healing comes from within and reclaim your power to direct your healing journey. Set boundaries, make decisions that honour your well-being, and take responsibility for your emotional and spiritual health.

- Balance Light and Shadow: Embrace both the positive

and challenging aspects of your journey. Healing isn't just about focusing on the good; it's about accepting and integrating all parts of yourself, including those that may be difficult to face.

- Stay Committed: Healing is not a one-time event but an ongoing process. Stay committed to your journey by continuing to explore new practices, seek support when needed, and remain open to growth and transformation.

Self-Assessment Questions

Have you ever experienced the loss of a loved one with whom you had a complex and strained relationship? How did their passing impact your healing and transformation, and were there moments of vulnerability or connection that helped you process the deep emotions and grief?

Have you ever grappled with the complexities of adoption and the grief for a parent you never fully knew? How have you navigated healing and finding inner peace, and what has helped you honour both the pain and the love that remain?

Have you ever realized that true healing requires confronting your inner shadows and embracing your light? How have you navigated self-discovery, and what steps have you taken to reclaim your power and reconnect with your true essence?

Chapter 13

A Milestone

In the weeks that followed, there was a noticeable shift in the energy within our home. It was as if the air itself had changed, carrying with it a sense of anticipation and unease. My husband, taking my words to heart, decided to embrace this new chapter in his life. He got himself a new wardrobe, a fresh haircut, and even set up a dating profile. It was clear he was ready to explore the freedom he now had to seek companionship elsewhere.

As the initial dust settled and the reality of our new dynamic began to sink in, I found myself wrestling with the consequences of my decision. There was a sense of liberation, yes, but it was also coupled with the stark and uncomfortable truth of my own displacement. I was no longer just a wife; I was now a guest in the life we had built together, a life that was steadily shifting away from me.

For the last three years of our marriage, I had been sleeping alone, silently yearning for the courage to voice my deep sense of loneliness. That empty bed had become a symbol of the disconnection that had seeped into our relationship, and more painfully, it was a stark reminder of my ongoing pattern of

Chapter 13 A Milestone

self-abandonment. I had been so focused on maintaining peace and avoiding conflict that I had neglected my own needs, pushing them to the background in favour of keeping up appearances.

The reality of this struck me hard. The bed I slept in was more than just a physical space; it was a reflection of the emotional chasm that had grown between us, and within myself. My own silence had been a form of betrayal—betrayal of my desires, my needs, and ultimately, of my own sense of worth. The courage I had wished for, to speak up and reclaim my place in my own life, was something I was only now beginning to confront. And it was this very realisation that marked the beginning of my journey back to myself, rediscovering my voice and reconnecting with the parts of me that I had long ignored.

Within three weeks my husband was dating somebody else. A "what the fuck just happened" moment, like a bomb had gone off inside of me and an absolute disbelief that my partner of thirty years is doing exactly what I said to do! Within months we were living separately, and a divorce asked for by my husband within the year.

It took me a long time to reconcile but I am filled with gratitude for the man who had the courage to release me from the chains of my own making. For it was his strength and conviction that paved the way for my own liberation, allowing me to step into the fullness of my power and reclaim my sense of self. There is no way I would have had the courage to leave.

Strong beliefs that marriage is death do us part and the guilt of splitting up our family was not a path I would take. I would sacrifice my own happiness for my family.

Gone were the days of wishful thinking and clinging to empty hopes. I let go of the futile aspirations that had once held me captive, and instead, I embraced a radical acceptance of my emotions, my reality, and my deepest desires. There was no more yearning for a love that had long faded, no more dreaming of a connection that simply no longer existed. To continue longing for something that was gone would be to deny the very essence of who I was and what I needed.

In choosing to honour my own truth, I unlocked a newfound sense of freedom and empowerment. It wasn't about seeking validation from anyone else; it was about embracing myself—flaws, scars, and all—with unwavering self-acceptance. This shift in perspective was nothing short of transformative. I began to see love, marriage, and the human experience in a completely new light.

Love, I realised, isn't about losing yourself in someone else or conforming to an ideal that no longer serves you. It's about recognising your own worth and understanding that true connection starts from within. My marriage, once a symbol of security and stability, had become a reflection of compromise and self-sacrifice, where my own needs were often neglected. But in this new chapter, I saw it for what it truly was—a journey, not a destination. It was an experience that had shaped me, taught me, and ultimately led me back to myself.

Chapter 13   A Milestone

As I embraced this new understanding, I felt a sense of liberation that was deeply personal. It was the kind of freedom that comes from knowing you are enough just as you are, without needing anyone else to complete you. This realisation changed everything. It redefined my relationship with myself, allowed me to set boundaries with confidence, and gave me the courage to pursue a life that was authentically mine.

The path wasn't without its challenges. There were moments of doubt, fear, and loneliness. But through it all, I remained committed to my own growth, knowing that the path I was on was the right one for me. In the end, it wasn't about the loss of a marriage or the end of a chapter—it was about the birth of a new one, where I was the author of my own story, and my happiness was firmly in my own hands.

Organizing my 50th birthday party was a significant milestone in my life. As someone who had rarely celebrated birthdays or focused on myself, it was a declaration of self-worth and a turning point in my life. For years, I had poured my energy into others, often neglecting my own needs and desires. This time, I was determined to celebrate my life and the progress I had made. It was time to acknowledge my struggles, and my triumphs. I wanted my 50th birthday to be memorable, so I planned an elaborate celebration.

I hired the largest limousine available and invited 13 of my closest friends, including my sisters and my childhood friend from New Zealand. Their presence was particularly meaningful to me. My sister, born of my adoptive parents, had become a steadfast support for me, especially during the tumultuous years of transition. Her life had not been easy, and I can say that her resilience and unwavering support have been a rock for me. My deep love for her was a constant source of strength and having her by my side for this milestone was incredibly special. A school friend whom I met when I was just 13, also played a crucial role in my life. Growing up, I often found comfort in her home, where her mother would always feed me. I suspect her mother knew that I wasn't being properly nourished at home, and her quiet generosity left a lasting impression on me. Her presence at my 50th birthday was a reminder of the enduring friendship that had sustained me through difficult times. She had tirelessly helped me through high school with explaining and supporting me in the classroom.

The night of the party was magical. We all piled into the limousine, the air filled with laughter and the clinking of champagne glasses. As we cruised into the city, I felt a sense of joy and liberation. We had dinner at a fabulous restaurant, and then we danced until dawn at a nightclub called the Brooklyn Standard in Brisbane. The night was a blur of fun and celebration, a perfect encapsulation of the spirit of the occasion.

The festivities didn't end there. My sister, school friend and I spent a week together, immersing ourselves in each other's company and making the most of the Gold Coast's offerings. We visited Versace, indulging in the luxurious surroundings and creating memories that would last a lifetime. One of the most significant aspects of my 50th birthday celebration was

Chapter 13   A Milestone

the gathering at a winery, where I brought together my entire family, including my sons' partners and my ex-husband. Despite our history and the end of our marriage, it was important for me to include him in this milestone. This gathering was more than just a party; it was a rite of passage, symbolizing the importance of family and the progress I had made in my personal life.

Reflecting on this milestone, I realized how much I had grown. Organizing and celebrating my 50th birthday was an act of self-love and recognition of my worth. It marked the end of a chapter filled with challenges and the beginning of a new era of self-acceptance and empowerment. The joy I felt throughout that week, surrounded by the people who mattered most to me, was a testament to the strength and resilience I had cultivated over the years. I had undergone significant personal transformation. I had confronted my past, dealt with my traumas, and worked tirelessly to heal. My 50th birthday was not just a celebration of my age, but a celebration of my journey, my resilience, and my unwavering commitment to personal growth.

The party had been more than just a celebration; it was a powerful reminder that it was never too late to celebrate oneself, to take centre stage in one's own life story. It had been an affirmation that I, too, deserved to be cherished, honoured, and surrounded by love—not just from others, but from within. It stood as a testament to the transformative power of self-love, a concept that had once felt foreign but was now becoming the bedrock of my existence.

The celebration had been about more than just marking another year; it was about recognising the milestones I had reached, the battles I had fought, and the strength I had discovered along the way. Each moment of the party had been infused with the lessons I had learned, the importance of honouring oneself, of taking the time to acknowledge the work I had put in, and of celebrating not just the destination, but the steps that had gotten me there.

As I moved forward into the next phase of my life, I had been filled with a sense of excitement and hope. There was a renewed energy within me, a drive to continue the exploration of self-discovery and self-celebration. The party had been a turning point, a moment when I had realised that the goal wasn't just about surviving, it was about thriving. It had been about embracing every twist and turn, every triumph and setback, with the knowledge that each one was a part of my story, and that story was worth celebrating.

With this newfound perspective, I stepped into the future with confidence, ready to honour myself and my journey in every way possible. I had been excited to see where this path would lead, knowing that as long as I continued to centre myself, to celebrate myself, and to embrace the lessons of my past, the possibilities were endless. The party had been just the beginning—a launchpad into a life lived fully, with intention, self-respect, and joy.

Healing in Practice

Celebrating milestones and celebrating yourself can be powerful acts of self-love and healing. Here are some healing practices associated with these concepts:

1. Personal Rituals

- Creating a Milestone Journal: Document significant moments in your life, noting what you've learned and how you've grown. Revisiting these entries can help you appreciate your progress and reinforce self-worth.
- Self-Ceremony: Design a personal ceremony to mark important milestones, such as lighting candles, meditating, or creating art. This ritual can be a sacred space to honour your achievements and set intentions for the future.

2. Self-Reflection

- Reflective Writing: Write letters to your past or future self, acknowledging your journey, expressing gratitude, and setting goals. This practice can help you process emotions and celebrate your evolution.
- Gratitude Practice: Regularly list things you're grateful for, especially those related to your personal growth. This helps shift your focus to positive experiences and accomplishments.

3. Mindfulness and Meditation

- Guided Meditations for Self-Love: Use meditations specifically designed to foster self-love and appreciation, helping you connect with your inner worth.
- Mindful Celebration: During milestone events, practice mindfulness by being fully present, noticing your emotions, sensations, and thoughts. This can deepen your appreciation of the moment.

4. Artistic Expression

- Creative Milestone Art: Paint, draw, or craft something that represents your journey or a specific achievement. This creative outlet allows you to express and celebrate your emotions tangibly.
- Vision Boarding: Create a vision board that reflects your goals and the milestones you want to celebrate in the future. This visual tool can inspire and motivate you.

5. Community and Connection

- Celebrating with Loved Ones: Host a gathering with friends and family to celebrate your achievements. Sharing your joy with others reinforces your sense of belonging and self-worth.
- Storytelling Circles: Join or create a group where people share their life stories and milestones. This practice builds community and validates your experiences.

6. Body-Centred Practices

- Movement Rituals: Engage in dance, yoga, or any movement that makes you feel alive and connected to your body. Celebrate milestones by moving in ways that express joy and gratitude.
- Spa Day or Body Care Rituals: Treat yourself to a spa day or create a self-care ritual at home, such as a long bath or massage. This practice honours your body and helps you feel nurtured.

7. Nature-Based Celebrations

- Nature Walks or Retreats: Spend time in nature to reflect on your journey. Use the natural environment as a metaphor for your growth, drawing parallels between your personal milestones and the cycles of nature.
- Planting a Tree or Garden: Plant something as a symbol of your growth. Watching it grow can be a powerful reminder of your own resilience and achievements.

8. Affirmations and Positive Reinforcement

- Daily Affirmations: Create affirmations that celebrate your milestones and strengths. Repeating them daily helps reinforce positive self-beliefs.
- Affirmation Jar: Write down your achievements and positive traits on slips of paper and place them in a jar.

On challenging days, read through them to remind yourself of your worth and progress.

9. Milestone Tokens

- Creating or Wearing Symbolic Jewellery: Choose or create a piece of jewellery that symbolizes a milestone. Wearing it can serve as a constant reminder of your achievements.
- Keepsake Box: Collect mementos from your milestones—photos, letters, small items—and keep them in a special box. Revisiting these items can help you reconnect with your journey.

10. Acts of Service

- Giving Back: Celebrate your milestones by giving back to others, such as volunteering or mentoring. Helping others can deepen your sense of purpose and fulfillment.
- Paying It Forward: In honour of your achievements, perform random acts of kindness. This spreads positivity and reinforces your connection to the world around you.

Incorporating these practices into your life can help you honour your journey, celebrate your growth, and reinforce a deep sense of self-worth and well-being.

Self-Assessment Questions

Have you ever planned a significant celebration for yourself as a declaration of self-worth?

How did this experience impact your journey of acknowledging your struggles and triumphs?

What can you do in the future to celebrate you and bask in your uniqueness and awesomeness.

Chapter 14

Spending Addiction

Turning 50 was a milestone that brought with it a mix of reflection, celebration, and a surprising confrontation with my sense of wealth and self-worth. The decade leading up to it had been a whirlwind of grief and transformation. It was a time when life threw relentless challenges my way, forcing me to navigate emotional storms and significant changes. But by the time I hit 50, the intensity of that grief had finally started to ease.

One of the events of that year was the arrival of a substantial sum of money from my divorce settlement. Suddenly, my bank account was looking healthier than it ever had, but rather than feeling secure or happy, I was hit with a wave of complex emotions that caught me off guard.

Wealth had never been something I associated with myself. Growing up, money was tight, and I'd always been taught to work hard and live within my means. So, when this money appeared, it didn't feel like mine, it felt foreign, like "dirty money" that I hadn't really earned or deserved. The discomfort was almost palpable, making me question my own worth and how I saw myself in the world. I found it easy to spend, I

Chapter 14   Spending Addiction

needed to dispose of it as I felt unworthy of it and every dollar was a reminder of something unresolved within me.

Instead of bringing the freedom or relief I might've expected, the money stirred up old wounds and insecurities about who I was and what I was worth. It became clear that this wasn't just about finances—it was about confronting deeper issues of self-worth and my relationship with abundance.

I began spending the money as quickly as possible. I bought a big, flashy house and indulged in luxury items. I purchased an expensive Cavoodle puppy, took my youngest child on an extravagant trip to America and Canada, and even bought a convertible. It was as if I couldn't spend the money fast enough. Each purchase was a subconscious attempt to rid myself of this wealth that felt so undeserved. At the time, I didn't understand why I was behaving this way. Now, I see that I lacked financial maturity. My husband had always provided for us beautifully. He managed our finances, ensuring that I never had to worry about money. My own work contributed, but it was not essential for our financial stability. This dependence and my upbringing in scarcity and neglect left me financially immature and unaware of the true value of money.

The sense of unworthiness that drove my spending spree was deeply rooted in my past. Growing up, I had never been taught to value money. I had always lived in survival mode, scarcity thinking focusing on immediate needs rather than understanding financial security or long-term planning. This mindset carried over into my adulthood. Despite the outward appearances of success and stability, I never truly felt deserving of financial abundance.

As I settled into my new rental, finding solace in the familiar comforts of Netflix and a glass of red wine, I was forced to confront the reality of my co-dependency and the deep impact it had on my life. For years, I had convinced myself that I was empowered, that my self-esteem was solid, but now it was clear that beneath that facade lay a heart weighed down by dependency and fear.

My eldest son, perhaps sensing the gravity of the situation, chose to live with me in the rental. His decision wasn't just about staying with me; it was also a search for stability, a way to escape the chaos of our old family home and find a new way forward. Meanwhile, my middle son decided it was time to strike out on his own, seeking the independence that comes with stepping away from the nest.

But it was my youngest who presented the biggest challenge. With his father still living in the family home, the idea of splitting his time between two households was a source of tension and uncertainty. The last thing I wanted was to put him through the emotional tug-of-war that can come with moving back and forth between two homes. I knew it could cause more harm than good, so I made the tough decision to insist that he live with me full-time. It wasn't an easy choice, but it was one I felt was necessary to protect his well-being.

In those early days, surrounded by the walls of my new home, I began to peel back the layers of my own behaviour. I

Chapter 14 Spending Addiction

saw how much of my life had been shaped by a need to please, to avoid conflict, and to hold onto a sense of security—even when that security was just an illusion. The rental, small and unassuming, became more than just a roof over my head; it became a space for reflection, healing, and rebuilding.

I started to see that this was an opportunity—a chance to truly step into my own power, to let go of the old patterns of dependency that had held me back for so long. It was a time to redefine what strength and independence really meant, not just for me, but for my boys as well. I wanted to show them that it was possible to rebuild, to find your footing even after the ground has shifted beneath you.

Even as I did my best to protect my children from the fallout of our separation, there were challenges I never could have anticipated—challenges that threatened to unravel the delicate balance we had worked so hard to achieve. One particular incident still stands out vividly in my memory as a moment that forced me to confront parts of myself I hadn't known existed.

It happened one ordinary afternoon, in the house that had been our family home for seventeen years. My ex-husband's new partner made an unexpected appearance, right there in the home where my children were. The shock of it hit me like a ton of bricks, and before I knew it, a volcanic anger erupted within me—a rage so intense and overwhelming that it felt like it might consume me entirely. It wasn't just the presence of another woman in the home that set me off; it was the sudden, jarring intrusion into the fragile world I was trying to rebuild for my children.

For years, I had been the model of composure. I had buried my emotions deep, hiding them under layers of restraint and a calm exterior. But this? This was different. It felt like a direct attack on the well-being of my kids, a risk that could throw them into even more emotional turmoil and confusion during an already difficult time. And that was something I simply couldn't tolerate.

In that moment, something primal and powerful surged up from within me. I was no longer just reacting; I was protecting. I tapped into a wellspring of strength and resolve that I never knew I had. All those years of holding back, of being polite, of putting on a brave face for the sake of peace—those years dissolved in an instant as I stood up for my children and their need for security.

It was a turning point for me, a moment when I realised that my power wasn't in keeping everything together on the surface, but in embracing the full range of my emotions—even the ones I'd been taught to suppress. I understood then that protecting my children sometimes meant stepping into that fierce, untamed part of myself, the part that wouldn't stand idly by while their world was threatened.

That day, I learned that there's a time and place for restraint, but there's also a time for fierce, unapologetic action. And in standing up for my kids, I wasn't just defending their security—I was reclaiming a part of myself that I had long denied. It was a moment of reckoning that forced me to confront the depths of my own strength and resilience. As I stood my ground, advocating fiercely for the safety and security of my children, I realized that I no longer needed to rely on others for validation or support. I was enough on my own. I was a force to be reckoned with, capable of protecting and nurturing my family with unwavering devotion and love. In choosing to prioritize my children's welfare above all else, I reclaimed my agency and embraced my independence in a way I never thought possible.

Despite the denial that had wrapped itself around my life like a protective blanket, I started to feel the slow, yet undeniable, stirrings of change within me. It was as if the layers of my old self were peeling away, making room for something new to emerge. Much like a chick breaking free from its shell, I began to break through the confines of my co-dependency, cautiously stepping into a world that was tinged with both uncertainty and possibility. The volatile arguments that had once defined our relationship and my relentless need to please were no longer enough to anchor me to the life I had always known.

I soon came to realise that true liberation wasn't something that could be given or found externally; it had to be forged in the crucible of grief. For those who have never experienced the end of a long-term marriage, the depths of this grief may seem unimaginable—a shadowy abyss where light and hope feel permanently out of reach. But for me, this grief was not just an emotion to be endured; it was a rite of passage, a sacred and necessary rite of passage into the very heart of my own pain and despair.

This was not a grief that could be easily shaken off or glossed over. It was a grief that demanded my full attention, my complete surrender. It required me to face the darkest corners of my soul, to confront the fears and insecurities that had kept me tethered to a life that no longer served me.

In allowing myself to fully experience this grief, I began to unearth the deeper truths that had been buried beneath years of denial and self-deception. I discovered that the end of my marriage was not just the loss of a partner, but the loss of an identity I had clung to for so long. It was the death of the person I had been, and the birth of someone new—a version of myself who was stronger, more resilient, and no longer defined by the need to please others.

As I navigated this painful terrain, I realised that the grief I was experiencing was not something to be feared, but something to be embraced. It was a transformative force, one that had the power to reshape my entire life. In grieving the loss of my marriage, I was also grieving the loss of the woman I had been—the one who had lived in the shadows, who had feared stepping into the light of her own truth.

But in this grief, I also found the seeds of my own rebirth. I began to see that the end of my marriage was not just an ending, but a beginning—a chance to rewrite the story of my life on my own terms. The tendrils of change that had begun to wind their way through my soul were not just pulling me away from the past, but guiding me toward a future filled with possibility and hope.

This sacred pathway through grief became the crucible in which my new self was forged. It was painful, yes, but it was also profoundly healing. Through it all, I came to understand that true liberation—true freedom—could only be found by facing the darkest parts of myself and emerging on the other side, not unscathed, but transformed.

This chapter of my life taught me that wealth is not just about financial assets, but about the richness of experiences, the depth of relationships, and the strength of character. It reminded me that true worth comes from within, and that believing in oneself is the foundation of genuine prosperity. As I continue to move forward, I carry these lessons with me, embracing both the challenges and the triumphs with a renewed sense of purpose and self-worth.

Healing in Practice

This period of reckless spending was a painful but necessary lesson in self-worth and financial literacy. I began to see how my beliefs about money were intertwined with my sense of self-worth. I had to confront the uncomfortable truths about my relationship with money and the deep-seated feelings of inadequacy that fuelled my actions. This experience of self-discovery was not easy, but it was essential for my growth. Through this process, including a financial planner, counsellor, journalling, self-reflecting and podcasts I started to develop a healthier relationship with money. I learned to see it not as a measure of my worth, but as a tool that could be used wisely and thoughtfully. I began to educate myself about financial management and made a conscious effort to change my spending habits. This shift was not just about money—it was about recognizing my own value and believing that I was worthy of abundance and prosperity.

For years, I struggled with feelings of unworthiness and a reluctance to embrace wealth. Despite accumulating wealth with my ex-husband over three decades, I never felt truly deserving of it. But now, after delving deep into the recesses of my soul and reclaiming my sense of self-worth, I was ready to step into my power and create my own wealth. This newfound sense of inner wealth, forged through years of introspection and emotional healing, has laid the foundation for outer wealth. No longer shackled by self-doubt, insecurity, spending when I was bored, lonely or unhappy I now possess the clarity and confidence to pursue financial abundance with purpose and intention.

But this transformation didn't happen overnight. It required an inner shift that could only occur through facing my deepest fears and confronting the wounds of my past. Through the support of my siblings and the guidance of mentors, I continued with self-discovery, learning to manage my emotions, master mindfulness, and, most importantly, meet the true essence of who I am. I understood that true wealth is not merely measured in material possessions or financial assets. It is found in the depths of our being, in the richness of our inner world, and in the sense of fulfillment that comes from living authentically and purposefully.

With inner wealth, I have a new sense of gratitude and reverence for the experiences that have brought me here. My inner wealth is the wealth of self-knowledge, self-love, and self-acceptance and will continue to guide me on this path of abundance and fulfillment.

Resolving an unhealthy relationship with money involves addressing both the practical and emotional aspects of your financial life. Here are some additional strategies:

1. Identify and Challenge Limiting Beliefs

- Belief Mapping: Create a map of your core beliefs about money. Identify where these beliefs originated (e.g., childhood experiences, societal messages) and evaluate whether they serve your current financial goals. Replace limiting beliefs with empowering ones.
- Therapy or Counselling: Work with a therapist, especially one who specializes in financial or cognitive-behavioural therapy, to explore deep-seated issues around money. Therapy can help uncover and resolve unconscious patterns that affect your financial decisions.

2. Cultivate a Healthy Money Mindset
- Mindset Shift: Start viewing money as a tool for empowerment rather than a source of stress, control or guilt. Reframe your perspective to see money as a resource that can support your well-being, personal growth, and the pursuit of your passions.
- Visualize Abundance: Engage in regular visualization exercises where you imagine yourself living a life of financial abundance and security. Picture yourself making wise financial decisions and feeling at ease with your finances.

3. Practice Financial Self-Care
- Regular Financial Check-ins: Schedule monthly financial reviews to assess your spending, savings, and investment goals. Treat these check-ins as an act of self-care, recognizing that managing your finances is a way to care for your future self.
- Set Clear Financial Goals: Define clear, achievable financial goals, whether it's building an emergency fund, paying off debt, or saving for a major purchase. Having specific goals helps focus your efforts and provides motivation.

4. Create Healthy Money Habits
- Automate Savings: Set up automatic transfers to your savings account or investment portfolio. Automating

savings ensures that you're consistently building financial security without having to think about it.
- Mindful Spending: Before making a purchase, pause to consider whether it aligns with your financial goals and values. Practice asking yourself questions like, "Does this bring me joy?" or "Is this a necessary expense?"

5. Educate Yourself Financially

- Invest in Financial Literacy: Read books, attend seminars, or take online courses on personal finance. The more knowledgeable you are about money, the more confident and empowered you'll feel in making financial decisions.
- Track Your Spending: Use apps or budgeting tools to track your spending habits. Understanding where your money goes can help you make adjustments that align with your financial goals.

6. Reframe Debt and Financial Mistakes

- Shift Perspective on Debt: Instead of viewing debt as a burden, see it as a learning opportunity. Develop a plan to manage or pay off debt and celebrate progress along the way.
- Forgive Past Mistakes: Everyone makes financial mistakes. Acknowledge past errors, learn from them, and let go of any associated guilt or shame. Use these

experiences as a foundation for better decision-making in the future.

7. Incorporate Mindfulness and Gratitude
- Mindful Money Practices: Incorporate mindfulness into your financial routines. For example, when paying bills, take a moment to be grateful for the services you receive in exchange for your money.
- Gratitude for Wealth: Regularly practice gratitude for the financial resources you currently have, whether they're large or small. Gratitude can shift your focus from what you lack to what you already possess, fostering a more positive relationship with money.

8. Create a Money Vision Board
- Visual Representation of Goals: Create a vision board that represents your financial goals and the life you want to build. Include images, words, and symbols that inspire you and remind you of your financial aspirations.

9. Seek Financial Independence
- Side Income Streams: Consider creating additional streams of income, such as freelancing, investing, or starting a small business. Financial independence can enhance your sense of security and reduce anxiety about money.

- Emergency Fund: Build an emergency fund to cover at least three to six months of living expenses. Having this safety net can ease financial stress and give you more freedom in your financial decisions.

10. Surround Yourself with Positive Influences
- Community and Mentorship: Surround yourself with people who have a healthy relationship with money. Seek out mentors who can provide guidance, share experiences, and help you stay accountable to your financial goals.
- Positive Financial Media: Consume financial content (books, podcasts, blogs) that promotes a healthy, empowering relationship with money. This can reinforce positive beliefs and practices in your financial life.

Self-Assessment Questions

Have you ever recognized that financial dependence impacted your maturity with money? How did addressing your sense of unworthiness and financial habits become a lesson in self-worth and financial literacy?

How have you come to understand that true wealth encompasses more than financial assets? What experiences have taught you that self-belief and inner worth are the foundations of genuine prosperity?

Have you ever experienced an inner shift through facing

your deepest fears and past wounds? How did the support of loved ones and mentors help you on your journey of self-discovery and mindfulness?

Chapter 15

Sexual Awakening

For years, I pushed my own desires aside, burying my instincts under the weight of what society and marriage expected of me. I put my well-being on the back burner, convincing myself that it was just part of the deal. But as I waded through the choppy waters of separation and divorce, one truth became impossible to ignore: the most important act of self-love is not to abandon yourself.

It hit me like a bolt of lightning—each time I went along with physical intimacy when my heart wasn't in it, I was betraying myself in the deepest way possible. It was like I was trading away my own dignity, doing something that felt as wrong as it did empty. Every time I gave in to my ex-husband's advances out of duty or fear, I was turning my back on what I really needed and wanted. I was denying myself the basic right to honour my own feelings and desires. And that's a line I should never have crossed.

As I began to step out from the shadows of my old life, I found myself on a path of self-discovery and liberation. There was this deep, almost primal urge to reclaim my autonomy, my sense of self, and my right to make decisions that truly reflected who I was. I threw myself into understanding the ins and outs of marriage and relationships, and that's how my podcast, "Empowered Marriage," was born. It became my outlet to dive into the complexities of love, intimacy, and self-acceptance, not just for my listeners but for myself as well.

Around that time, a couple of my girlfriends started nudging me towards dating again. The thought of it was utterly overwhelming. I had only ever been with one man—my ex-husband. As our marriage came to an end, I found myself questioning everything, including my own sexuality. The whole idea of dating felt foreign, like something from another world. It was filled with uncertainty and anxiety, and I wasn't sure if I was ready to navigate it.

It was as if the end of my marriage had opened up this Pandora's box of doubts and questions. Who was I now? What did I want? And could I really put myself out there again after all these years? The prospect of dating was daunting, but it also held the promise of new beginnings, of discovering parts of myself that I had long forgotten. And so, even with all the fear and uncertainty, I started to consider it. Slowly, tentatively, I began to imagine what it might be like to explore this new chapter of my life, on my terms, with a deeper understanding of who I was and what I truly wanted.

Life threw me an unexpected curveball. I'd developed a polyp in my throat from all the talking I'd been doing in hypnotherapy sessions, which eventually required surgery. It was like my body was telling me, "Enough is enough, it's

Chapter 15   Sexual Awakening

time to slow down." So, I decided to take a step back and give myself a break after the operation. I headed to the Sunshine Coast, booking a stay at a charming little Airbnb to recharge.

On the second morning of my retreat, I found myself in a quaint coffee shop, enjoying a quiet moment with a hot cup of coffee. It was one of those peaceful, rare moments where I could just be with myself, letting the world drift by. Then, out of nowhere, I noticed him—a man with deeply tanned skin, clearly someone who spent a lot of time outdoors, and muscles that looked like they belonged on a billboard. He must have been around 35, definitely younger than me by a fair bit.

Our eyes met, and before I knew it, he was walking over and striking up a conversation. There was something easy and natural about the way we clicked, despite the obvious age gap. It wasn't just small talk either—there was a genuine, comfortable rhythm to our conversation, like we'd known each other for ages. When I mentioned I was about to order breakfast, he casually asked if he could join me. I didn't think too much of it at the time and agreed, naively unaware of where this unexpected encounter might lead.

After breakfast, I had plans to go for a swim and, without thinking much of it, invited him along. I was still blissfully unaware of any romantic undercurrents—I just thought it'd be nice to have some company. We drove separately to this stunning, secluded spot I knew of, one of those hidden gems where the world seems to stand still.

The swim was everything I needed—refreshing, calming,

like washing away layers of stress and doubt. As we floated together in the water, something began to shift inside me. It was subtle at first, like a flicker of something I hadn't felt in years. The scene couldn't have been more perfect if it was scripted. Rain started to softly fall, and a rainbow stretched across the sky, creating this surreal, almost magical atmosphere. Before I knew it, we were hugging, and then, out of nowhere, we kissed. It was my first kiss with another man in over three decades, and it felt like a jolt of electricity coursing through my body, awakening parts of me that had been dormant for so long.

We laid on the beach afterward, just soaking in the moment. The intensity of it all—the kiss, the rain, the rainbow—was almost too much to process. I felt alive in a way I hadn't in years, like something inside me had finally clicked back into place. After a while, the practical need for food brought us back down to earth, so we decided to grab lunch together. But the magic of that morning, the connection we shared, lingered in the air like a warm, comforting blanket. He suggested a more private spot, and by then, the stirring inside me made me agree.

We drove to a secluded location, where we shared a deeply intimate experience that didn't include sex but did involve oral sex. This encounter was nothing short of transformative. It was as if a part of me that had been dormant for years had suddenly come alive. For three weeks, we maintained an intense, passionate connection, even though I had to return home. I was aware that he was a player and that our fling wouldn't last, but I didn't mind. He had given me a gift. It was an awakening.

Reflecting on those weeks, I realize how pivotal this experience was for me. It was a beautiful gift and a reminder of my own vitality and capacity for joy. This encounter awakened something within me that had long been buried under layers of grief and self-doubt. It was a powerful, life-affirming experience that reignited my sense of self and opened me up to new possibilities. After emerging from my period of grief, I felt a stirring within me—a yearning to explore, to connect, and to embrace life anew. At 51, I decided I was ready to date for the first time in my life. Having never dated before, the prospect was both thrilling and terrifying. The world of dating apps was an uncharted territory, and diving into it felt like stepping into a different reality.

I started with an app called Plenty of Fish, which I quickly dubbed "a brothel on legs." The app was notorious for its ease of access to casual encounters. If I wanted to meet someone for sex that night, I could. The power of choice was exhilarating; I felt in control of my own destiny, reclaiming a part of myself that had been dormant. But this intense energy became an addiction. I found myself constantly seeking the next thrill, the next high. The moment I started using these apps, it was as if a floodgate had opened. I felt like an 18-year-old again, filled with boundless energy and a desire to experience everything life had to offer. I even joined an intense fitness program to channel my newfound vitality. The energy was intoxicating and overwhelming even.

The dating apps became my playground: Plenty of Fish, Bumble, Elite Singles. I juggled multiple conversations, each promising a different kind of excitement. The allure of these encounters was irresistible and also a bit reckless. If I am honest, I sometimes neglected safety in my pursuit of these experiences. At one point, I dated a man who still lived with his ex-wife. We would have dinner in the city and then retreat to the back seat of my car. It was behaviour I would have never imagined myself engaging in, but I was living out a teenage fantasy I never had the chance to explore.

This period of my life strained many of my friendships. Many ended, particularly with a dear friend who had been a part of my life for 20 years. On reflection, I constantly sought her approval and refrained from speaking honestly, fearing rejection and disapproval from the maternal energy she embodied. When I finally did speak up, she rejected me, and we were unable to reconcile our differences. As a result, our friendship ended. It was a painful loss, but I was in a state of rebirth, and I needed to prioritise self-discovery over the expectations of others. Reflecting on my youth, I realized I had never had a chance to explore this side of myself. My brother's death when I was young had pushed me towards choosing security over personal and sexual awakening. Now, this long-suppressed part of me was bursting forth with a vengeance. It was a wild, uncontrollable rebirth, and for six months, I surrendered into it.

Chapter 15   Sexual Awakening

One Sunday night was the turning point. It was 11:30 PM, and I found myself driving around, trying to find a house where I was supposed to meet someone. I didn't even have his house number, and as I aimlessly drove down the street, peering into cottage-style houses, a wave of realization hit me. What was I doing? The absurdity and recklessness of my actions struck me like a bolt of lightning. It was the wake-up call I desperately needed after six months of risky behaviour. The next day, the man messaged me, explaining that he had fallen asleep and that's how little regard this most vulnerable act of my body meant to him. But by then, it didn't matter. The shock of that night had interrupted my descent into chaos and brought clarity. I realized I needed to take control in a healthier way, to channel my newfound energy and desire for life more constructively.

This wild period of rebirth had been crucial. It had allowed me to reconnect with my deepest desires and to discover parts of myself I never knew existed. But now, it was time to integrate these discoveries into a balanced life. I learned that true inner wealth comes from knowing and accepting all parts of oneself, even those that emerge in unexpected and uncontrollable ways.

My closest sister had some idea about my wild behaviour during my period of awakening, but no one knew the full extent of it. My dear friend, from whom I had distanced myself, had inklings too. Another sister was somewhat aware, but the depth of my actions remained largely hidden. It reached a point where I realized I needed serious help to regain control and purpose in my life. A significant aspect of my sexual addiction was the "hunt" for sex, driven by a compulsive need to seek out and pursue new sexual partners or experiences. The anticipation and pursuit of a new sexual partner produced a heightened sense of excitement and adrenaline for me, which I found addictive. The act of pursuing and "conquering" a new partner gave me a temporary sense of achievement and validation. Over time, I needed to engage in more frequent or riskier pursuits to achieve the same level of excitement.

Determined to change, I sought out a coach, specifically a male coach, with purposeful intent because I had not experienced a male coach or counsellor before. Working one-on-one with him for several months provided immense value. He helped me navigate my chaotic energy and channel it into something more constructive. I paused all dating and focused on reconnecting with myself, slowing down, and reassessing my life's direction. During this transformation, I made a significant decision. I booked a spot at ISTA, the Institute School of Temple Arts in the Blue Mountains, for a 7 day live in workshop that was scheduled for six months later.

I felt ready to re-enter the dating world with a new perspective after working with my coach. I changed my dating profile significantly, becoming very clear about the type of relationship I sought and the values I held. No longer interested in casual encounters, I was ready for a committed relationship. This clarity filtered out the undesirables, leaving only those who

Chapter 15 Sexual Awakening

resonated with my new vision. I chose to use Bumble, an app where women initiate contact. It was there that I came across a man who immediately grabbed my attention. It was on my ex-husband's birthday when I first saw his photo, and I felt it was a sign. There was something grounding and solid about him that resonated deeply with me. We started texting, and within a few days, we had arranged to meet.

I found myself yearning for a different kind of relationship. One grounded in mutual respect, love, and understanding. The bumble man I met—my partner of five years now—was someone I had to grow into. If I hadn't done the inner work, I would still be chasing after the wrong kind of partners, stuck in a destructive pattern. I firmly believe that the universe conspired to bring us together once I was ready. Two weeks before I met him, I had a sense that he was close. Every day, I would sit in my room and visualize the kind of man I wanted to be with. I wrote detailed entries in my journal, describing his qualities, our interactions, and the life we would share. I visualized him in my home, in my bed, and in my life. This wasn't a desperate hope but a calm assurance that he was already energetically present.

When I finally saw his profile online, it felt entirely natural, almost like a homecoming. Meeting him wasn't a surprise or a stroke of luck; it was the fulfillment of a manifestation. I had already embodied the relationship I wanted, so when he appeared, it was simply the universe aligning with my intentions. This experience taught me the power of clarity and intention. By becoming crystal clear about what I wanted and embodying those desires, I created the conditions for them to manifest in my life. It wasn't about hunting or chasing; it was about becoming the person who would attract the kind of partner I desired.

When we finally met, it was at Elysium Restaurant, a charming spot that added to the magic of our first encounter. I remember the moment I saw Russ. His hand-knitted jumper immediately setting him apart from the 'bad boys' of my past. There was a solidity and grounding about him that resonated deeply with me. He had brought a single rose, placing it gently on the table in a gesture that spoke volumes about his thoughtfulness and sincerity. Our conversation flowed effortlessly, and I felt an immediate connection. This wasn't just about physical attraction; it was about a deeper, more powerful connection. For the first time, I trusted my body's signals completely, allowing my intuition to guide me. This was a testament to my growth, learning to use my body as a vessel for discernment.

Our second date at Wellington Point by the water further solidified our connection. The beautiful setting mirrored the serenity and beauty I felt inside. I knew then that I had found someone special. His patience, gentleness, and genuine nature were exactly what I needed. I realize that meeting him was a milestone in my personal transformation. It symbolized my rebirth and the fulfillment of a new chapter in my life, one grounded in authenticity, love, and deep connection. It was the culmination of years of work, unravelling old patterns, and stepping into my true self. This chapter of my life taught me that true love isn't something you find; it's something you create within yourself first. By becoming the person, you want to be, you attract the kind of partner who matches that energy. And when you meet that person, it feels like coming home.

I left him to go on my retreat with an immersive, experimental workshop focused on shamanism, sexuality, and spirituality. It was a humbling experience, peeling back layers of my identity and forcing me to confront deep-seated issues. There were about 100 participants, most of whom were in their 20s, 30s, and 40s. Only a handful, including myself, were over 50. Honouring the sacred space of the workshop, I can't divulge the details, but it was transformative. I came back to him ready to commit into our future.

Five years have passed since our first meeting, and we are still together and very much in love. This relationship has been a testament to my self-discovery and transformation. It symbolizes my rebirth and the fulfillment of a new chapter in my life, one grounded in authenticity, love, trust and deep connection.

Healing in Practice

Managing sex addiction requires a multi-faceted approach that combines professional support, self-awareness, and healthy lifestyle changes. Here are some practical ways to manage sex addiction:

1. Seek Professional Help

- Therapy: Engage in therapy with a licensed professional, such as a sex addiction therapist or a psychologist specializing in addiction. Cognitive Behavioural Therapy (CBT) can be particularly effective in addressing underlying issues and changing harmful patterns of thought and behaviour.
- Support Groups: Join a support group like Sex Addicts Anonymous (SAA) where you can connect with others who are experiencing similar challenges. Sharing your experiences in a safe environment can be incredibly beneficial.

2. Establish Boundaries

- Identify Triggers: Work with your therapist to identify the triggers that lead to addictive behaviour. These might include stress, loneliness, or specific situations that prompt compulsive sexual thoughts or actions.
- Create a Plan: Develop a clear plan for avoiding or managing triggers. This might include avoiding certain places, people, or situations that are associated with your addiction.

3. Develop Healthy Coping Mechanisms

- Mindfulness and Meditation: Practice mindfulness techniques to become more aware of your thoughts

and urges without acting on them. Meditation can help you develop greater control over your impulses.
- Exercise: Regular physical activity can help reduce stress and anxiety, which are often underlying causes of addictive behaviour. Exercise also helps to refocus energy in a positive direction.
- Healthy Hobbies: Engage in hobbies or activities that provide fulfillment and distraction from sexual urges, such as painting, writing, gardening, or volunteering.

4. Manage Technology Use
- Digital Detox: Limit your use of technology, especially if certain apps, websites, or online environments are linked to your addiction. Consider using apps that block access to triggering content or set limits on your screen time.
- Accountability Software: Install software that tracks your online activity and reports it to a trusted accountability partner, helping you stay on track.

5. Build a Support Network
- Trusted Friends and Family: Open up to trusted friends or family members about your struggle. Their support can be invaluable as you navigate your recovery journey.
- Accountability Partner: Work with an accountability partner who can check in with you regularly, offering

support and encouragement while holding you accountable to your recovery goals.

6. Focus on Emotional Health
- Address Underlying Issues: Work through any underlying emotional or psychological issues that may be contributing to your addiction, such as trauma, depression, or anxiety.
- Practice Self-Compassion: Be gentle with yourself during your recovery. Recognize that setbacks may happen, but they don't define your progress. Celebrate your successes, no matter how small.

7. Set Realistic Goals
- Small Steps: Recovery is a journey, not a destination. Set small, achievable goals and celebrate your progress along the way.
- Regular Reflection: Regularly assess your progress with your therapist or support group, adjusting your strategies as needed.

8. Create a Balanced Lifestyle
- Routine: Establish a daily routine that includes time for work, leisure, socializing, and self-care. A balanced lifestyle reduces stress and creates a sense of normalcy.
- Healthy Relationships: Focus on building and

maintaining healthy, non-sexual relationships that provide emotional support and connection.

9. Education and Awareness

- Learn About Addiction: Educate yourself about sex addiction, understanding that it's a recognized condition that requires treatment. Knowledge can empower you to take control of your recovery.
- Stay Informed: Stay informed about the latest research and treatment methods related to sex addiction. This can help you feel more in control and optimistic about your recovery.

10. Emergency Plan

- Crisis Plan: Have a plan in place for what to do when you feel overwhelmed by urges. This could include calling a therapist, reaching out to a support group, or using a coping strategy like deep breathing or going for a walk.
- Sex addiction is challenging, but with the right support and strategies, it is manageable. Recovery is a personal journey, and finding what works best for you is key to achieving long-term success.

Self-Assessment Questions

Do you feel that partnering early in life caused you to miss out on exploring your sexuality? How has this realization impacted your journey of self-discovery and personal fulfillment?

Have you ever felt a sense that the right partner was close, after doing significant inner work? How did visualizing and manifesting your ideal relationship impact your readiness to embrace love and mutual respect in a new partnership?

Have you ever found yourself diving into new experiences with a sense of excitement and recklessness? How did the thrill of these adventures help you reclaim parts of yourself, and what did you learn about balancing safety and desire in the process?

Chapter 16

Losing Lily

Russ and I were fully invested in each other, and our relationship had blossomed to the point where we knew it was time to make a big commitment—buying a home together. He had been living with me in my house, but we decided to sell it and find a place that truly felt like ours. On my birthday in November 2021, we moved into a beautiful home by the water—a dream I'd held onto for 15 years. This wasn't just any house; it was the one I had envisioned on my dream board, something I'd worked hard to manifest.

I first laid eyes on this house years ago, and I felt an instant connection. Back then, it was just out of reach financially, and it didn't quite meet all my needs. It didn't have a front room for my counselling practice, and the yard was non-existent, making it impractical at the time. Still, there was something about it that kept pulling me back, like it was waiting for the right moment to become mine.

When Russ and I began house hunting, I kept this vision in my heart. One night, I saw the house listed online, and something inside me clicked. The very next day, we bought it. It felt like destiny, like every step we had taken led us precisely to this moment. The timing was perfect, and so was the house. We moved in during November, and the transition was filled with joy and anticipation. Our home by the water was everything I had dreamed of and more. We planned to throw a housewarming and New Year's party to celebrate our new beginning, marking the end of one chapter and the start of another.

December swept in with all its usual bustle, but this year it felt different—there was an extra layer of excitement as we prepared for our first big gathering in the new house. This wasn't just a regular holiday get-together; it was a celebration of everything new in our lives—new beginnings, new hopes, and a new chapter in a place that already felt like home.

We had planned every detail meticulously, wanting the event to be perfect. The house was decorated, the menu was set, and we were ready to welcome friends and family into our dream home. On the 29th of December 2021, just two days before the big celebration, Russ and I decided to take a quick trip to Gympie to visit his mum. It was meant to be a short, joyful visit—just a brief break before the party.

As we pulled out of the driveway, the holiday spirit was in full swing. We were chatting, laughing, and feeling on top of the world, proud of how smoothly everything had come together. I absentmindedly picked up my phone, thinking it would be wise to check for any last-minute messages or updates about the party. But instead of the usual texts about food or timing, I saw a message that stopped me cold. It was

Chapter 16 Losing Lily

from Lily's kids' stepmum, and I could tell by the tone that it wasn't just a casual note.

In an instant, the carefree mood of the day evaporated. My heart raced as I opened the message, feeling a sense of dread that I couldn't quite place. The words on the screen were the last thing I expected, and they hit me like a ton of bricks. The festive bubble we'd been in burst, replaced by a wave of anxiety and curiosity. I turned to Russ, my voice shaking as I told him about the message, knowing that whatever was in it was about to change everything.

"I'm really sorry to give you this bad news, but Lily has passed away."

Lily took her own life on Owen's birthday. To try and comprehend this over a text message was unbearable and shocking. Lily, my baby sister, had been a constant in my life as a child and young adult, a source of love and strength. The news hit me like a physical blow. In an instant, the joy and excitement of our new beginning were overshadowed by the sudden and overwhelming grief of her loss. It was a moment of shock and sorrow, one that would forever mark that December. Lily had chosen to end her life.

As we continued our drive, the excitement of the holiday season quickly faded into the background. The party, the decorations, the anticipation—they all seemed so distant, overshadowed by a sudden, overwhelming wave of grief. My thoughts were consumed by memories of Lily—her infectious laughter, her unwavering support, and the countless moments we'd shared over the years.

The new house, which just hours earlier had felt like a beacon of hope and a fresh start, now seemed empty and hollow in her absence. It was as if the very foundation of our new beginning had shifted, leaving me unsteady and unsure. The juxtaposition of joy and sorrow was almost too much to bear, the conflicting emotions swirling inside me like a storm I couldn't control.

By the time we arrived at Russ's mother's house, I was physically present but mentally elsewhere. Every smile, every word spoken felt like it was happening in a haze, as if I were watching from a distance. My mind kept replaying moments with Lily, desperately trying to grasp the reality that she was truly gone. I was in shock, the weight of the loss pressing down on me with a force I hadn't anticipated.

The party we had meticulously planned—the one that was supposed to be a celebration of new beginnings—now felt trivial, almost insignificant in the face of such loss. The thought of hosting people, of pretending everything was okay, seemed impossible. All I could do was try to navigate the early stages of grief, fumbling through the motions of life while my heart ached with the realization that I would have to move forward without my sister.

In those moments, I realised that overcoming grief is never straightforward. It's messy, unpredictable, and deeply personal. The shock, the disbelief and the sorrow don't come with a roadmap or a timeline. They hit you when you least expect it, reshaping your reality in ways you never imagined.

Chapter 16   Losing Lily

And as much as I wanted to retreat, to hide from the pain, I knew I had to face it head-on, just as I had faced every other challenge in my life. But this time, it would be different. This time, it was about learning to live without someone who had always been there, about finding strength in the memories, and about somehow finding a way to honour her legacy in a world that suddenly felt much emptier.

My relationship with Lily had shifted dramatically over the years, evolving from the close bond we once shared to something much more complicated. As time went on, boundaries became essential—not just for maintaining a sense of peace in my life, but for safeguarding my own well-being.

The turning point came after our mother passed away in 2016. Losing Mum was devastating for both of us, but it hit Lily particularly hard. Her life took a sharp turn for the worse, and before long, addiction had taken its relentless grip on her. I tried, really tried, to be there for her. I reached out, offered support, and did my best to show her love in the way she needed. But addiction is a powerful force, one that often creates walls between even the closest of loved ones.

Over time, it became clear that I couldn't save Lily from her struggles, no matter how much I wanted to. The more I tried to help, the more I found myself getting pulled into a vortex of anxiety, stress, and emotional exhaustion. It was heartbreaking to see someone I loved so much spiral out of control, but it became increasingly clear that I had to make a choice. I had to prioritize my own mental and emotional health.

Making the decision to distance myself was one of the hardest things I've ever done. I felt an immense sense of guilt, as though I was abandoning her in her time of need. But deep down, I knew that if I didn't establish those boundaries, I would lose myself in the process. I needed to protect my own well-being, to find a way to live without constantly being consumed by worry and fear for Lily.

Even with the distance, Lily was never far from my thoughts. Every time I caught a glimpse of her life through others, I felt a mix of emotions—relief that I was no longer in the thick of it, but also a deep, lingering sadness for the sister I had lost long before she was truly gone.

In those years, I learned a lot about the delicate balance between loving someone and taking care of yourself. Sometimes, the most loving thing you can do—for both yourself and the other person—is to step back, even when every part of you wants to rush in and fix things. It's not easy, and it's not without pain, but it's necessary.

As I sat in Russ's mother's house, trying to process the news of Lily's death, all these memories came flooding back. The guilt, the grief, the relief—all mixed together in a confusing jumble of emotions. I knew that I had done what I needed to do, but it didn't make the loss any easier to bear. The boundaries I'd set for my own well-being hadn't just protected me; they had also created a distance that now felt impossible to close.

I vividly remember the last time I saw Lily. It was at our mother's funeral, a day already heavy with grief and loss. As

Chapter 16   Losing Lily

we stood side by side, saying our final goodbyes to Mum, I couldn't help but notice the toll that addiction had taken on Lily. Her once vibrant spirit seemed dulled, her eyes clouded by the lies and destructive patterns that had come to dominate her life. It was painfully clear to me, even in that moment of shared sorrow, that the path she was on was one that I couldn't follow—not if I wanted to preserve my own values.

In the days, weeks, and months that followed, I wrestled with the decision to step back. It wasn't something I took lightly. How do you distance yourself from a sister, someone who shares your history, your memories, and your bond? But as much as it hurt, I knew I had to protect myself. Lily's spiralling addiction had created a whirlwind of chaos, and I wasn't going to be pulled in. The lies, the erratic behaviour, the constant worry—it was too much. I needed to draw a line for my own sake.

Over the years that followed, there were occasional messages exchanged between us. Each one carried a weight of its own, a mixture of hope that she was turning a corner and the dread of what I might hear next. But the reality was that the distance between us only seemed to grow wider. Every message reminded me of the sister I was losing to addiction, and every silence echoed with the unspoken understanding that things were getting worse.

It wasn't that I didn't want to help. Every fibre of my being wanted to reach out, to pull her back from the brink, to somehow fix what was broken. But I had come to a painful realization: I couldn't save Lily if she wasn't willing to save herself. No matter how much I loved her, no matter how strong my desire to help, the truth was that she had to want to change. And until that day came, if it ever did, there was nothing I could do.

This realization left me grappling with feelings of guilt and helplessness. What kind of sister was I if I couldn't be there for her? But as time went on, I began to understand that this wasn't about me failing her. It was about setting boundaries as I couldn't sacrifice my own well-being in a futile attempt to rescue my sister who wasn't ready to be saved.

I carried this guilt with me, though, like a shadow. It was always there, lingering at the edges of my mind. Every time I heard about Lily, every time I thought of her, there was that pang of regret—could I have done more? Should I have tried harder? But deep down, I knew I had made the right choice, no matter how difficult it had been. I had to protect myself, to preserve the life I had built, even if it meant letting go of someone I loved.

As I sat in that car, driving away from Russ's mother's house, the memories of Lily flooded back, a mix of love, sadness, and confusion. I wished things could have been different, that she could have found her way out of the darkness. But I also knew that I had to find a way to forgive myself, to accept that sometimes, the hardest decisions are the ones we make to protect our own hearts. And in that moment, I realized that the grief I was feeling wasn't just for Lily—it was also for the

Chapter 16 Losing Lily

sisterhood that we had lost along the way.

The Māori community at Waimarama Beach welcomed Lily, even thou she was Samoan, with open arms, offering her a dignified and beautiful farewell that honoured her spirit in a profound way. Despite the challenges posed by COVID-19, they ensured that Lily's farewell was conducted with the utmost respect and reverence. In the Māori tradition, death is not seen as an end, but rather a continuation. Lily's passing was embraced as a natural part of life, and her departure was marked by a ceremony filled with love, respect, dignity and deep cultural significance.

Her ex-partner and his partner, along with her three children, played a pivotal role in transporting Lily back to Waimarama Beach, where she would be laid to rest near the ocean she loved so dearly. In a testament to the strength of community and the power of cultural tradition, they held an open casket ceremony in their own home, allowing family and friends to pay their respects and honour Lily's memory. For me, witnessing the beauty and grace of Lily's farewell on zoom due to covid was both heartbreaking and healing. While I may not have agreed with her choice to leave this world, I found peace in knowing that she was surrounded by love and respect in her resting place.

In the wake of the COVID-19 pandemic, the collective trauma that permeates our society has become more palpable than ever before. From the fear that hangs heavy in the air to the rising tide of domestic violence, suicide, mental health, economic hardship to name a few it's clear that we are living in a world where suffering lurks around every corner. But what exactly is trauma, and how does it impact our lives? For many, trauma is a word shrouded in mystery that haunts the recesses of our minds, leaving us feeling overwhelmed and powerless. But in reality, trauma is far more pervasive than we may realize.

At its core, trauma is the residue of experiences that leave us feeling unsafe and vulnerable. It can be as simple as a break up with a school friend or as complex as witnessing our parents' tumultuous fights. And though the events themselves may vary, the impact is the same—trauma lodges itself in our bodies, leaving us feeling overwhelmed and disconnected from ourselves. For many individuals and adoptees, trauma takes on a unique dimension, as they navigate the complexities of being severed from their biological roots and thrust into a world of uncertainty and instability. From an early age, adoptees are forced to grapple with feelings of abandonment and loss, their young minds unable to fully comprehend the depth of their pain.

Trauma does not discriminate. Whether it's the stoic silence of a young boy taught to suppress his emotions or the quiet desperation of a woman living in fear of her abusive partner, trauma leaves its mark on us all. And yet, despite the prevalence of trauma in our lives, there is hope—a pathway to healing that begins with acknowledging the pain that lies buried within us. It requires us to confront the wounds of our past, to cry, yell, and jump up and down and process until the trauma is finally expelled from our bodies.

Lily may have left this world, but her spirit lives on, forever etched in the hearts of those who knew and loved her. Farewell, dear sister. May you find peace and tranquillity in the eternal embrace of Waimarama Beach.

Healing in Practice

As I reflect on Lily's life and the impact she had on those around her, I'm reminded of the depth and resilience of the human spirit. Despite all the struggles, the pain, and the chaos that seemed to envelop her life, Lily's spirit remains a beacon—a light that still guides us toward understanding, compassion, and forgiveness. It's a light that shines on, even after she's gone, reminding me that love and connection can transcend the most challenging circumstances.

In our new home, I felt a deep need to honour Lily in a way that felt both personal and meaningful. So, I created a shrine dedicated to her, a space where her memory could be celebrated and kept close to our hearts. I adorned it with vibrant red hibiscus flowers, their bold colour and lively energy reflecting Lily's vibrant and free-spirited nature. The hibiscus, so rich in symbolism, also nods to her Samoan heritage, a connection that Lily always cherished.

This small shrine has become more than just a memorial; it's a daily reminder of Lily's presence in our lives. Every time I pass by it, I feel a sense of peace, knowing that, in some way, she's still with us. The love we shared, the bond of sisterhood, and the memories of happier times are all encapsulated in this space. It's a place where I can reflect, grieve, and, most importantly, remember the love that continues to bind us together, even in her absence.

Creating this shrine has been a deeply healing process for me. It's allowed me to channel my grief into something tangible, something that honours Lily's memory while also acknowledging the complex and often painful reality of our relationship. It's a space where I can confront the feelings of loss and sadness but also celebrate the joy and light that Lily brought into our lives.

As I sit quietly by the shrine, surrounded by the vibrant hibiscus, I often find myself reflecting not just on Lily's life but on the lessons she left behind. Her life, though fraught with difficulty, has taught me so much about the power of compassion, the importance of forgiveness, and the enduring strength of the human spirit. And in these moments of reflection, I find myself filled with a deep sense of gratitude—for the time we had together, for the love that persists, and for the ways in which Lily continues to inspire me, even now.

Lily's spirit, captured in the vibrant reds of the hibiscus, continues to be a source of strength for me as I move forward. It reminds me that even in the face of loss, there is always room for love, for connection, and for the kind of deep, abiding bond that transcends the physical world. And as I carry her memory with me, I know that she will always be a part of my life, guiding me with her light and her love.

Self-Assessment Questions

Have you ever received unexpected news that changed your life and emotions in an instant? How did you cope with the overwhelming grief and shock, especially when it overshadowed a moment of joy and new beginnings?

Have you ever had to set difficult boundaries with a loved one to protect your own well-being? How did you balance feelings of guilt and love, and what did you learn about the importance of boundaries for maintaining stability and peace?

Have you ever lost a loved one whose spirit continues to live on in your heart? How do you find ways to honour their memory and find peace during your grief?

Chapter 17

Soul Awakening

In the days and weeks that followed, Russ was my absolute rock. He was there with the support and understanding I needed so desperately. The house by the water, which once felt like a dream come true, took on a whole new meaning. It became my sanctuary, a place to retreat, mourn, and remember Lily. The beautiful views and the calm that once filled me with such joy now served as a quiet escape—a bittersweet reminder of how unpredictable life can be, where the happiest moments can suddenly collide with the deepest heartache.

Grief is such a strange and messy thing. It's a heaviness that wraps itself around your soul, almost suffocating, draining every bit of energy and joy you once had. It's like hope just disappears, and time feels like it's dragging on without any purpose. But at the same time, grief shows just how much we loved, how deeply we cared, and how much the people we've lost really meant to us.

In those early days of mourning Lily, I found myself wrestling with these mixed feelings. On one hand, I was completely consumed by the pain of losing her, feeling like a part of me was missing. On the other, the very fact that I was

Chapter 17   Soul Awakening

grieving so intensely was proof of how much she meant to me and how much she'd shaped my life.

Russ got this — probably better than anyone. He didn't try to fix the pain or offer up clichés that would've fallen flat. Instead, he just stayed close, giving me the support I needed, whether that meant holding me while I cried or simply sitting with me in silence. In those moments, I realised that even in the deepest pits of grief, I wasn't alone. The love and support of the people around me, especially Russ, became my lifeline, pulling me back when the sadness threatened to swallow me whole.

The house, which had been just a dream for so long, now felt like a symbol of resilience. It became the place where I started to piece my life back together, where I could slowly begin to find my way through the fog of grief. The water, always moving and changing, felt like a perfect metaphor for the grieving process—sometimes calm, sometimes stormy, but always moving forward.

As I spent more time in our new home, I started to see that grief, while incredibly painful, is also part of healing. It allowed me to honour Lily's memory, to feel the emptiness her loss had created, and to begin, ever so slowly, to mend my broken heart. I knew the journey ahead would be tough, full of ups and downs, but with Russ by my side and the strength I'd gained from this experience, I knew I could handle whatever came next.

In the quiet moments by the water, I came to realise that life is all about balance—the joy and the sorrow, the dreams we achieve and those we lose. And as I continued to grieve for Lily, I made a promise to myself: to cherish the happy moments when they come, to hold onto the memories of those I love, and to keep moving forward, even when the road is uncertain.

But as the weight of grief and fatigue pressed down on me, I knew something had to change. Burnout had taken hold, and with the thought of returning to work creeping closer, I felt an urgent need to get on top of my well-being. I couldn't keep going like this; something had to give.

Determined to make my healing a priority, I decided to take a bold step back from the daily grind and head off on a retreat. It wasn't just about getting away; it was about diving deep into a space where I could truly focus on myself, away from the noise and pressures of everyday life. I found a retreat nestled in a tranquil cabin by a peaceful stream, the perfect spot to unwind and reconnect with myself. For a whole week, I gave myself permission to fully surrender to my grief, to feel every bit of the pain without holding back or judging myself.

In the past, I'd been quick to push down my emotions, trying to move on before I was really ready. But this time, I was determined to do it differently. I went in armed with the lessons and tools I'd picked up through my struggles over the years. I was ready to face my pain head-on, knowing that the only way through it was to really allow myself to feel it.

It wasn't easy—far from it—but it was exactly what I needed. I embraced the process, knowing that this time I

Chapter 17 Soul Awakening

wasn't just going through the motions. I was fully committing to my healing, no matter how tough it got. The retreat gave me the space to really sit with my grief, to reflect, and to start the slow process of rebuilding my strength. It was a turning point, a chance to recharge and reconnect with myself in a way I hadn't done before.

I made a conscious decision to truly sit with my pain, to embrace the darkness instead of running from it. Decades earlier, when Owen took his own life, I buried that grief so deep that I never really allowed myself to feel it, let alone heal from it. I pushed it down, tucked it away, and tried to move on without ever confronting the hurt. For so long, I'd sought comfort in the arms of others, using relationships as a way to escape the turmoil brewing inside me. But now, there was no escaping it. Alone in my pain, I had nowhere to hide and no one to lean on but myself.

I let myself sink into the depths of my pain, confronting the demons that had been lurking in the shadows for far too long. It wasn't easy. It was a raw and harrowing experience, taking me to the darkest corners of my soul where the pain was almost unbearable. But for the first time, I faced that darkness with unwavering courage and resolve, determined to finally feel and heal.

The grieving process was anything but smooth. It was slow, drawn out, and at times felt like it would never end. Every day was a struggle, each step forward met with an equal pull backward. It was a crucible of transformation, testing me in ways I never imagined. But as I look back on those days, I see them as a turning point when my true strength and resilience were formed.

I am eternally grateful for that pain, even though it was the hardest thing I've ever done. It taught me that facing our pain head-on, no matter how terrifying it may seem, is the only way to truly heal. It showed me that I have the strength to navigate life's darkest moments and come out the other side not just surviving, but thriving.

Leaving the retreat was both a homecoming and a challenge. While I had found a sense of peace within myself, the return to the outside world brought with it a wave of uncertainty and the familiar feeling of disconnection from my body. Struggling to stay grounded in my body, but now knowing what it felt like to be present in my body, I sought further support through intensive counselling sessions with Robyn Pearson. Through her guidance, I learned to navigate the process of landing and coming home. Staying back into my body was an essential step towards wholeness. With each session, I felt myself sinking deeper into my body, reclaiming a sense of presence and embodiment that had long eluded me. It's not just about surviving anymore; it's about thriving despite the scars that once defined me.

The catalyst for my post-traumatic growth was a jolt that shook me to my core and forced me to confront the patterns that had kept me trapped for so long. I had always looked outside of myself for validation, for approval, for a sense of worthiness that I believed could only come from others. But in my darkest moments, I realized that true healing begins from within. It was a shift from seeking external validation to embracing my own inner wealth. The path forward became clear: I had to turn inward, to face the shadows that haunted me, and to reclaim the power I had unwittingly surrendered to others.

It wasn't easy. It isn't meant to be. Anyone who says any different is trying to sell you something. It demands courage to confront fears of rejection, to dismantle the old patterns of seeking validation through external measures and letting go. I had to learn to trust in my own worthiness, independent of others' opinions or expectations. Slowly, as I immersed myself in continued self-discovery and personal growth, I began to cultivate a deep sense of inner wealth. It wasn't about material riches or external successes; it was about the richness of my own self-acceptance, self- love, and self-trust. These were the treasures that no one could take away from me, no matter what life threw my way.

The process was transformative. I discovered the power of embodiment—of being fully present in my own body and mind. Instead of looking outside for validation, I learned to listen to the wisdom that emanated from within. This shift in perspective liberated me from the cycle of seeking external approval and allowed me to embrace authenticity and vulnerability. Today, as I write these words and share my lived experience as a coach and speaker, I stand in a place of transformation. The fear of rejection that once gripped me has dissipated because I have come to understand that my worthiness does not depend on others' acceptance of me. If someone rejects me now, it no longer shatters me, because I will never reject myself.

The house and Lily's passing are forever linked in my memory. This home, which had been a dream for so many years, became not just a fresh start with Russ, but a sanctuary where I could honour Lily's memory and work through my grief. It's as if this house was always meant to be more than just a place to live. It became a space where I could truly confront my past, grieve my losses, and begin to heal in a way I had never allowed myself to before.

Discovering inner wealth is a continuous exploration of growth, resilience and finding my true worth. It has led me to embrace my authenticity fully, to celebrate my strengths and acknowledge my vulnerabilities without shame or hesitation. Grounded and fully present in my body, I reflect on the events and people that have brought me to this moment. Though the road ahead may still be uncertain, I carry with me a newfound sense of resilience, inner peace, and a deep understanding of inner wealth. This inner power source, this wealth of my own making, was created as the push of pain and the pull of purpose worked in parallel. Trusting the process was the key that unlocked it.

Chapter 17   Soul Awakening

Healing in Action

The retreat provided a fertile ground for awakening. In the embrace of nature's serenity, I began to unravel the layers of sorrow that had accumulated within me. Each moment of introspection and reflection brought me closer to a deeper understanding of myself and the path to healing. One of the pivotal aspects was the willingness to engage in practices that encouraged the flow of energy within me. Whether through therapeutic touch or guided exercises, I allowed myself to be vulnerable, inviting others to connect with me on a profound level. In those moments of connection, I felt a stirring within me—an awakening of the spirit that had long lay dormant.

The retreat, with its breathtaking beauty and serene ambiance, provided the perfect backdrop for my self-discovery and healing. Though the retreat came at a cost, both financially and emotionally, it proved to be a priceless investment in my well-being and a testament to the transformative power of self-care and self-compassion. The retreat became a pivotal moment in my healing and a sanctuary where I could uncurl the layers of grief and begin the process of reclaiming myself. Engaging in various practices, from astrology, lomi lomi massage to facial therapy, I sought help and guidance in gentle modalities that nurtured both my body and spirit.

Physical activities like yoga, stretching and nourishing meals, journalling, self-reflecting provided a foundation, offering moments of respite amid the storm of emotions. As I slowly began to thaw from the freeze of shock, I found release in the presence of kindred spirits who listened with empathy and understanding, their silent support a balm for my wounded soul. Cut off from the distractions of the outside world, the retreat offered a rare opportunity for introspection and self-reflection. With no phone signal to tether me to the chaos of daily life, I surrendered to the depths of my grief, allowing myself to be fully present with the pain.

In the embrace of nature's tranquillity, I experienced moments of peace and love as well as a reminder that even amidst the darkest of times, there is light to be found. Though the weight of loss still hung heavy in my heart, I discovered a sense of contentment and acceptance that transcended the pain. As I emerged from the retreat, I carried with me a newfound sense of strength and resilience and a testament to the healing that had happened within me. Though the road ahead remained uncertain, I faced it with a renewed sense of purpose and a deep-seated belief in the power of healing and transformation.

Self-Assessment Questions

Have you ever reached a point of burnout that required you to take decisive action for your well-being? How did stepping back from daily demands help you restore your sense of self and find healing?

Have you ever found a sanctuary or retreat that became a pivotal point in your healing journey? How did engaging in various healing practices and connecting with kindred spirits help you regain strength and resilience?

Chapter 17   Soul Awakening

What steps can you take to engage in self-reflection, seek support, embrace vulnerability, and pursue your passions in order to foster post-traumatic growth and inner strength?

Chapter 18

Inner Wealth

As I sit down to write the final chapter of this book, I want to have a real, heart-to-heart chat with you, the reader. Looking back, I'm struck by the incredible journey of self-discovery and healing I've been on. What started out as an effort to make sense of my relationship with my sister Lily and my experience of adoption has grown into something much bigger than I ever imagined. My life has been one of inner transformation and awakening, and now, more than ever, I feel that my purpose is to share what I've learned with others.

When I first began writing this book, I was driven by thoughts of Lily. Her tragic passing shook me to my core, forcing me to confront the deep well of grief and the old wounds I hadn't yet faced. It felt like everything was about her, about the adoption, and all the complex emotions tied up with those experiences. But as I dug deeper into my own mind and heart, I realised it was about so much more. It wasn't just about Lily or adoption; it was about confronting the darkest corners of my soul, the parts I'd kept hidden, and then finding a way to step into the light of self-awareness and empowerment.

Chapter 18   Inner Wealth

Perhaps this inner knowing was something that began to take root in the early days of my childhood, during a time when even the simplest tasks—like walking and talking—were monumental challenges. Those formative years were tough, no doubt about it. But they were also the years where I first learned the value of perseverance and determination, traits that would become the bedrock of my resilience.

Looking back, I can see how those early struggles laid the foundation for the person I am today. Each small victory, each hard-fought milestone, planted a seed of strength within me—a seed that would grow and flourish as I faced the trials and tribulations of life. It's funny how life works sometimes. The very things that seem insurmountable at the time often end up being the crucibles in which our character is forged.

Growing up, I was surrounded by scarcity and uncertainty. I was a broken little girl, starved for love and acceptance in a world that seemed determined to crush my spirit. The wounds ran deep, leaving scars that would take decades to heal. Yet, amidst the darkness, there was a glimmer of potential waiting to be unleashed. What sets me apart from my siblings, who have not managed to find a way of uncovering and nurturing inner transformation? It's a question that I've grappled with many times, searching for answers in the depths of my soul.

Perhaps it was my innate resilience, a stubborn refusal to be defined by the circumstances of my upbringing. Even in the darkest moments, there was a spark within me—a knowingness that whispered, "You are meant to be here, and you are meant to be born and meant for more." Or maybe it was a combination of factors or a perfect storm of nature and nurture, circumstance and choice. I was fortunate to have mentors and guides along the way with people who saw the potential within me and nurtured it with love and encouragement.

But ultimately, I believe it was a conscious decision. It was a choice to confront my pain and to embrace my vulnerabilities. It was not an easy path to walk. My life has been filled with twists and turns, setbacks and triumphs. But with each step forward, I reclaimed a piece of myself, piecing together the fragments of my shattered past into a mosaic of strength and resilience. For me, self-discovery has been a lifelong pursuit. I have always been on a relentless quest to shed the layers of false identity and reclaim my true essence.

I can't help but acknowledge the stark contrast between the broken little girl I once was and the empowered woman I have become. It's a transformation that often leaves me in awe, as I reflect on my life and the strength I have found within myself. It's not just about surviving the hardships, but about embracing them as part of my story—part of what has shaped me into the person I am today.

What is it that allows some of us to rise from the ashes of our past, while others remain trapped in the darkness? Is it sheer willpower, or is there something deeper at play—an inner knowing, a quiet voice that whispers, "Keep going"?

Through the process of writing and reflecting, I have come

Chapter 18 Inner Wealth

to understand that our story is not unique. It is a universal truth of human experience and the process of grappling with loss, confronting trauma, and ultimately, finding healing and redemption. At its core, this book is a testament to the power of inner work—the power of delving deep into the recesses of our souls and confronting the shadows that lurk within. It is about learning to embrace our vulnerabilities, confront our fears, and reclaim our sense of self-worth and purpose.

Why was I able to hold onto my inner wealth when my siblings were overcome by the relentless grip of mental health struggles? The answer, I think, lies in the power of inner knowing. This inner flame wasn't something I fully understood as a child, but it was always there, quietly burning away, giving me the strength to navigate whatever life threw my way. Where others might have faltered, that flame kept me going, reminding me that there was always something worth fighting for, something more to live for.

I've come to realise that this resilience, this inner wealth, isn't something we're simply born with—it's something we nurture, something we feed with every choice we make, every challenge we face. It's what's kept me grounded, what's allowed me to weather the storms of life while others have been swept away.

This book has taken me to places I never expected to go. It's taught me lessons I never thought I'd learn, and it's helped me understand myself in ways I never imagined. And now, as I bring this story to a close, I'm filled with a deep sense of gratitude for the struggles, for the breakthroughs, and for the chance to pass on what I've learned to you.

Suicide isn't just a single tragic event; it's a slow, creeping unravelling, a descent into darkness that feels almost impossible to climb out of. It is marked by the gradual loss of self, where bits of our identity slip away, leaving us feeling utterly lost in a sea of emptiness and despair. I've seen this unravelling up close—both in my own life and in the lives of those I've held dear.

Lily came into this world full of hope and possibility, a pure, loving soul who deserved nothing but the best life had to offer. But as the years went by, she found herself tangled in a web of desperation, yearning for love and acceptance in a world that seemed hell-bent on withholding both from her. It was heartbreaking to watch her struggle, to see the light in her eyes fade as she fought a battle she never should have had to fight.

To the outside world, Owen was just another lost soul, searching for his place in a world that couldn't—or wouldn't—give him the answers he needed. His story, like Lily's, is a stark reminder of how fragile we all are, how easily we can be pushed to the edge when life becomes too much to bear.

The pain of losing them is something that will never fully go away, but in telling their stories, I hope to shed light on the silent battles so many face. Because in the end, it's not just about the tragedy of their loss; it's about understanding what led them there, the struggles they endured, and the desperate

Chapter 18   Inner Wealth

need for compassion and connection in a world that often feels cold and unyielding.

Owen and Lily's stories are a familiar one. They are both about lost identity and fractured authenticity. Born into a world of false selves and fleeting facades, they struggled to find their true self amidst the struggles of their upbringing. And as they lost themselves, Lily's Samoan culture and Owen's Tongan culture, piece by piece, they found themselves spiralling further and further into despair. But their stories are not unique. In fact, it's emblematic of a larger trend that sees individuals and adoptees, particularly males, disproportionately affected by suicide. The statistics are staggering, painting a grim picture of a population that is struggling to find its place in a world that often seems determined to reject it.

And yet, I am still here. The same adopted family. The same upbringing. Why did I look towards the glimmer of light that pierced through the shadows that they could not see? It begins with a willingness to confront the false selves and wounded parts that have taken root within us, to dig deep and unearth the authentic self that lies beneath the surface. When I decided to write this book it was about them, but now I know it was for me.

It has been a process of excavation, digging through the layers of trauma and pain to uncover the buried treasure of my authentic self. And though the work is far from over, I am grateful for the progress I have made. I've learned to recognize the false selves and wounded parts as they arise, to hold space for them with compassion and curiosity. And in doing so, I've found a newfound sense of peace and acceptance and a sense of self that is rooted not in seeking validation from others, but in finding love and acceptance within myself.

But this road is not one that I walk alone. It is a journey that I share with others. This is healing and transformation that is deeply rooted in the power of human connection. And as I continue to walk this path, I am reminded of the words of one of my sisters, who once told me that healing is like a dog with a bone; you just keep digging and digging until you find what you're looking for.

And so, I continue to dig. I am digging through the layers of false identity and woundedness, seeking the buried treasure of my true self. And though the road ahead may be long and fraught with challenges, I walk it with hope in my heart, knowing that true healing is possible for those who are willing to try. And I invite you to walk it with me.

I am a master of manifesting and strive to be a beacon of hope for others. I am constantly reminded about the power of choice. We may not have control over the circumstances of our upbringing, but we do have control over how we choose to respond. In the end, it is our choices that shape our destiny, transforming what is broken into beauty, and pain into purpose. But there is more to it than just resilience. I believe that my ability to maintain inner wealth stems from a deep sense of connection—to myself, to my purpose, and to the world around me. This connection has been nurtured and strengthened over the years through introspection, self-discovery, and spiritual practice.

Through this process of deep self-reflection and growth, I've come to realise something significant about myself and those who are wired like me. I am a high achiever and perhaps you are - driven by a relentless pursuit of success and excellence. We are the ones who set the bar impossibly high, not just for others but, most of all, for ourselves.

But here's the thing—when we get out of balance, that drive can become our undoing. I know this all too well because when I lose my equilibrium, I tend to overachieve. I push harder, work longer, stay in my head and become almost obsessive in my pursuit of goals. It's an old pattern, one rooted in the need for external validation. We start seeking approval from the outside world, measuring our worth by our achievements rather than our peace and fulfillment.

This relentless drive can be both a blessing and a curse. On the one hand, it fuels our success and propels us forward, but on the other, it can lead to burnout, stress, and a disconnect from trust and our true selves. It's a delicate balance, and when it's tipped, it can throw our entire lives into chaos.

I've developed a framework called the **Push & Pull Method**—a roadmap specifically designed for high achievers like us to maintain balance and navigate life's ups and downs. The essence of this method lies in understanding the natural ebb and flow of our energy, our power source. It emphasizes connecting inwardly to your passion, purpose, and potential.

Recognising the push of pain and utilizing the skills, works alongside the pull of purpose, keeping you moving forward and aligned with your authentic self."

The Push & Pull Method isn't just about managing our time or setting boundaries—though those are certainly important aspects. It's about having an AWARNESS and being able to recognise what you are feeling and allowing it to be there with curiosity, compassion and care. It's about the ACCEPTANCE of our reality and getting out of the story in our head. Living with AUTHENTIC ACTION and knowing when to lean into our drive and ambition and when to honour our need for rest and reflection being aligned to your inner values.

By navigating this roadmap, high achievers can maintain their drive without burning out. They can continue to excel and reach new heights without sacrificing their well-being or losing sight of what truly matters. It's a way to stay connected to our purpose, to keep our inner fire burning brightly without letting it consume us.

This method has become a cornerstone of my coaching work, something I'm deeply passionate about sharing with others who find themselves on a similar path. It's not just about achieving more—it's about achieving more while staying whole, balanced, and true to ourselves. In this way, the Push & Pull Method is more than just a strategy for success; it's a blueprint for a life lived in harmony with our deepest values and desires.

While my siblings faced their own battles, I was fortunate

to have a sense of alignment—a knowingness that guided me through life's twists and turns. Even in moments of darkness and despair, I held onto the belief that there was a greater purpose to my existence, a reason to keep moving forward. And while I cannot fully explain why I possess this inner wealth while others do not, I am grateful for the gifts it has bestowed upon me. It is a beacon of hope in times of uncertainty, a source of strength in moments of weakness, and a reminder that even in the face of adversity, there is always a bridge forward to be found.

I carry with me the lessons learned and the wisdom gained. I am reminded that resilience is not just about weathering the storm, but about finding peace and purpose amidst the chaos. And so, I embrace my inner wealth with gratitude and humility, knowing that it is a gift to be cherished and shared with the world. As I bring this account of my life so far to a close, I am filled with gratitude for the love and support of my children, partner, siblings, friends and for the wisdom of mentors and guides who have walked alongside me. I acknowledge the resilience and strength that lies within each and every one of us. While the inner work is far from easy, it is undoubtedly worth it. For in the process of healing ourselves, we not only transform our own lives but also ripple out healing and transformation into the world around us.

As I step forward into the next chapter of my life, I do so with a renewed sense of purpose and clarity. I am no longer defined by my past or constrained by my wounds. I am empowered to create my own reality, to shape my own destiny, and to live a life of authenticity, abundance, and joy. And so, dear reader, I invite you to do your own inner work, to delve deep into your soul, confront your shadows and emerge into the light of empowerment. For it is through discovering our own inner wealth that we truly come home to ourselves, finding peace, fulfillment and purpose along the way. And if you need someone to walk beside you, I am here.

With love and gratitude,
Helen

Author Bio

Growing up in Hawkes Bay, New Zealand, Helen fostered a deep connection with nature and the joy of play. Adopted into a large diverse multi-cultural family, she always had a companion for play and possessed an insatiable curiosity about human behaviour. Helen was driven by a desire to unravel the mysteries of what makes herself and people tick, consistently seeing the inherent goodness and potential in those she encountered.

While on a working holiday in Australia, Helen made the decision to uncover her biological roots when she received a life-changing phone call. The news of her 18-year-old brother Owen's suicide redirected Helen's trajectory, plunging her into a tumultuous battle with anxiety, depression, PTSD, and a host of addictions.

Amidst her healing, Helen discovered a calling to support others, prompting her to establish her Counselling and Coaching business in 2008 and publish a book. However, it was after the ending of her 30-year relationship/marriage that her passion for working with couples truly ignited. Launching The Empowered Marriage Podcast and earning numerous marriage awards became pivotal aspects of her renewed focus.

In a cruel twist of fate, tragedy struck once more in 2021

when Helen's younger sister, Lily, tragically took her own life. Amidst the depths of her grief, Helen found herself drawn back to her original calling, recognizing that even in the darkest moments, her purpose of inspiring others remained steadfast.

Today, Helen is committed to her calling as a transformational coach, speaker and author. She passionately champions the belief that life isn't merely imposed upon us, but rather, it unfolds in a purposeful manner. Helen's mission is to inspire individuals to unveil their genuine, authentic selves, separate from the survival personality crafted for acceptance. This transformation creates room for their true identity and authenticity to emerge, allowing their soul's calling and the genuine meaning and purpose of their lives to shine through.

Contact Helen at helen@helenharrison.com.au

www.helenharrison.com.au

www.ingramcontent.com/pod-product-compliance
Lightning Source LLC
Chambersburg PA
CBHW022048290426
44109CB00014B/1029